SOCIAL POLICY

HEA ... ARE

Tina Lovell & Claire Cordeaux

Hodder & Stoughton

GROUP

To Joseph and Paul
C. C.

For Allan, who kept his patience when I took on yet more work!
T. L.

Orders: please contact Bookpoint Ltd, 39 Milton Park, Abingdon, Oxon OX14 4TD. Telephone: (44) 01235 400414, Fax: (44) 01235 400454. Lines are open from 9.00–6.00, Monday to Saturday, with a 24 hour message answering service. Email address: orders@bookpoint.co.uk

A catalogue record for this title is available from The British Library

ISBN 0 340 683619

First published 1999
Impression number   10 9 8 7 6 5 4 3 2
Year   2004 2003 2002 2001 2000

Copyright © 1999 Tina Lovell, Claire Cordeaux

Cover illustration by Alex Green
Typeset by Wearset, Boldon, Tyne and Wear
Printed in Great Britain for Hodder & Stoughton Educational, a division of Hodder Headline Plc, 338 Euston Road, London NW1 3BH by J. W. Arrowsmith Ltd., Bristol.

Contents

Acknowledgements

The authors would like to acknowledge the Msc in Social Research Methods at London Guildhall University and Suffolk County Council Social Services Department.

The publishers would like to thank the following for permission to reproduce copyright photographs:
Dundee District Libraries, p. 50, top; *Punch*, p. 61, bottom; Popperfoto, p. 70, bottom; PA News, p. 76, top; Life File, p. 103, top; Department of Health, p. 109, bottom; Department of Education and Employment, p. 137, top; Life File, p. 163, bottom; Mo Wilson/Format, p. 171, bottom.

CHAPTER 1

AN INTRODUCTION TO SOCIAL POLICY

It is important to make a distinction between a **social policy** and an **organisational policy**. A social policy is any policy that regulates the organisation and delivery of services or resource allocation in the society in which it has been developed. An organisational policy reflects an organisation's value base, ie the way it believes things ought to be. A social policy is usually broadly based and may have a number of objectives; and a variety of initiatives or strategies may be used to implement it. The study of social policy analyses how a society organises and delivers its social and welfare services.

A policy is a **statement of intent**. It contains a course of action that regulates the way a service is structured and delivered. Some policies are said to contain a hidden agenda that contains messages, values or actions that are not obvious or openly discussed.

Traditionally, social policy has been associated with income maintenance, health, education, housing and social services. Social policy concerns itself with issues that are political, economic and social, and that enhance the welfare of people with particular needs or problems.

There are a number of political **ideologies**, each of which views the content and implementation of policy differently.

The type of social policy adopted by a society will be dependent on its **model of welfare**. Social policy is often developed in response to a social problem or the needs of particular groups of individuals. The statutory, private and voluntary sectors all have a role in the implementation of policy. It would be too costly to provide all services for everyone, and so, to ensure that those most in need have access to services and resources, 'eligibility criteria' are established.

Social policy is influenced by politics, legislation, the media, service providers, the European Union, the general public, technology and charismatic figures. It has an impact on attitudes, beliefs, values, practice, the delivery of services, social problems, life chances, social structure, lifestyle and future policy.

The same policy might be implemented differently in England, Scotland, Wales and Northern Ireland.

Social policy: a definition

Right from the outset, it is important to make a distinction between the study of **social policy**, a social policy itself and an **organisational policy**.

- The study of social policy involves analysing how a society organises and delivers its social and welfare services.

    Examples: the Audit Commission's review of the delivery of services to those with mental-health problems, older people and the disabled. Its report was called *Community Care: Agenda for Action*. This review resulted in the 1991 Community Care Act. More recently, Sir Ron Dearing has led a number of reviews concerning the organisation, funding and delivery of education. These reviews have culminated in new legislation and policy.

- A social policy, on the other hand, is the term used to describe any policy that regulates the organisation and delivery of services or resource allocation in the society in which it has been developed.

    Example: the National Curriculum was the result of a review by Sir Ron Dearing, and it dictates how a school should approach the content and delivery of education for 5–16-year-olds.

- All organisations have policies that explain to their staff and users how they are going to operate. Some of these organisational policies are based on legal requirements and responsibilities, whilst others reflect the organisations' value bases, ie the ways they believe things ought to be.

    Example: an **equal opportunities policy** contains a **statement of intent** that demonstrates how an organisation will ensure equality of opportunity and deal with discrimination. In effect, it is an agreement that ensures that all those who come into contact with the organisation are treated with equal regard. This may be a legal requirement – eg Equal Pay Act 1970, 1975 and 1983, and the European Union's Equal Pay Directive – or, more commonly, it may reflect an organisation's own thinking on the subject.

activity

1 Collect together three equal opportunities policies:
   - one from a **statutory service**, eg Social Services or a healthcare trust;
   - one from a voluntary organisation, eg Help the Aged;
   - one from a private company, eg a college or Marks and Spencer.

   Compare the contents: how are they the same, how are they different? Do they reflect current legislation?

2 Look at the way the above policies have been written. In small groups, draw up an equal opportunities policy for your faculty or department.

WHAT IS A POLICY?

A policy is a statement of intent. In the case of social policy, it is society that is making the statement of intent, or rather it is the government and legislators/social administrators on society's behalf. It contains a course of action that in some way regulates one or all of the following:

- the way a service or an area of social life is structured and functions
- the delivery of services
- the actions of those working to deliver the service
- the way that resources are allocated.

In the main, social policies are those that broadly outline the way 'society' agrees things should be, in a given area of social life or social service.

Social policy: a hidden agenda

A *hidden agenda* is one that is not obvious. For instance, it is argued that a school operates two curricula. The first is the National Curriculum, which determines what is taught in schools and the content of those subject areas. The second, or hidden curriculum, conveys to pupils a set of values, principles and attitudes that promote conformity and thus ensure that society continues to function in much the same way as before. This is sometimes referred to as the status quo. Some social policies are accused of openly advocating one thing whilst containing a hidden agenda that achieves something else or something in addition to the stated intent. This is one reason why the study of social policy is important. Policy can be challenged and might even be changed as a result.

Social policy and social engineering

Our parents and carers are our primary socialisers: it is they who teach us how to live in society. Through them we get to know not only their own values, beliefs and opinions but also those of society at large. We learn about morals: distinguishing right from wrong, good from bad. We learn what behaviour is seen as desirable and in what situations. At two years of age, we can have a temper tantrum in a shop, lie on the floor and scream. If this were done at 22 years of age, it is likely that the police would be called! As we get older, other institutions such as schools take on some of the responsibility for promoting citizenship. It is believed that social policy has a lead role in maintaining social control. That policy itself dictates to society its expectations of the latter in order to maintain the status quo. This is sometimes called **social engineering**. Social policy determines the way a society

CASE STUDY

Immigration

Case 1:

The 1962 and 1971 Commonwealth Immigration Acts were about the admission of members of the Commonwealth into Britain and the maintenance of their dependants. The sole-responsibility rule in the 1971 Act laid down restricted conditions for single parents bringing their children to live with them in Britain. In order to do so, they had to prove that they alone had maintained their children and had kept regular contact with them, including visits. Fiona Williams (1989) asserts that this ruling was particularly discriminating for black women, many of whom had come to Britain at the request of the National Health Service. An acute shortage of nurses and ancillary staff had prompted a publicity campaign in the Caribbean, encouraging women to leave their children and come to Britain. Many of these women were low paid, making it extremely difficult for them to meet the sole-responsibility ruling. Whilst the Acts themselves were not overtly discriminating, their implementation was. Some would argue that the policy-makers knew this to be an outcome of the policy: the hidden agenda was to limit the number of Commonwealth immigrants without actually stating this openly.

Case 2:

Michael Hill, in his book *Social Policy: A Comparative Analysis* (1996), attempts to demonstrate that immigrants are denied citizenship rights, the rights of ethnic minorities being undermined by systems and measures controlling immigration. He argues that social policies often prioritise some cultural patterns and fail to recognise others. This form of discrimination contributes to the economic, political and social disenfranchisement of immigrants, including second generations born in Britain. This can lead to their being pushed into exploited positions, particularly when claiming benefits or seeking housing or employment. These controls have often adversely affected particular groups of immigrants, primarily black and Asian groups. Studies have revealed that black tenants occupy the worst council housing and that those who own their homes are often forced to buy near-derelict property because of the difficulties in getting a mortgage. In addition, black and Asian groups are often forced to pay higher interest rates to private companies because mainstream building societies fail to serve them (Fiona Williams, 1989). These results are not directed by immigration policy but are a result of its interpretation and implementation, coupled with indirect and sometimes direct racism. The 1976 Discrimination Act was an attempt to address some of the worst effects of racism, but the Commission for Racial Equality (CRE) was given very limited powers, and it is often difficult to prove discrimination. The growth in the use of equal opportunities policies has led to some progress in the last decade, but we still have some way to go.

organises itself and influences the behaviour of its citizens. In the 1980s, Margaret Thatcher introduced a set of policies that promoted a new vision of society. These policies 'engineered' a change in society's aspirations and attitude. These policies were developed over two decades, and many younger people grew up knowing no other policy or attitude. The phrase 'Thatcher's Children' has been used to describe them. This indicates the power that social policy can have over the thoughts and behaviour of both individuals and society.

Social policy: as a field of study

Social policy is the study of how a society organises and delivers its social and welfare services. It is a field of study rather than a discrete subject. This is because those who study it have a variety of reasons for doing so and come from different backgrounds. For instance, an economist might study social policy to find out what impact it has on the wealth of the citizens it affects or on society as a whole, **sociologists** study social policy to help them analyse how a society functions and organises itself; and **social administrators** study social policy to monitor its effectiveness. The studies of all these people might take the form of research, a review, a field study, market research, action research, consultation papers, reports or an inquiry.

Social policy covers a wide range of topic areas. Traditionally, these have been the social/welfare services, which include:

* income maintenance
* health services
* education
* social services
* housing.

These are often called the 'five pillars' of the **welfare state**, as it is in these areas of service provision that the state (or government) has become most involved.

Sociology and social administration have always played an important part in the study of these areas. Sociologists undertake research in an attempt to explain how and why societies have organised themselves and functioned the way they have. They want to see what effect the welfare state has on people's lives, and they try to establish reasons why policies are developed the way they are. Social administrators see their task as that of identifying and demonstrating areas of need in order to ensure effective service delivery and secure policy reform. Whilst sociologists give the reasons for social problems and social inequality, social administrators attempt to find solutions. Increasingly, other disciplines have begun to analyse social policy in an attempt to explain current trends or to advocate change in their own areas of interest. The study of social policy no longer confines itself to those areas of service provision traditionally associated with the welfare state. Issues related to race, gender and disability have become increasingly important. Fiona Williams (1989) argues that issues of race and gender have been marginalised or neglected in the study of social policy, resulting in the discrimination of certain groups in both the organisation and delivery of services.

Michael Oliver (1996) makes a similar case for people who are disabled. More recently, issues related to the environment, such as transport, pollution and conservation, have also been considered aspects of social policy. Over time, the concentration of study on service delivery has also changed. The study of social policy now includes discussion about the political and social attitudes that are predominant at the time policy decisions are made.

Why study social policy?

Paul Spiker (1995) suggests the following three reasons:

1 SOCIAL POLICY IS ABOUT POLICY

In essence, the study of social policy is concerned with the economic, political and institutional relationships involved in the development and implementation of policy, including service delivery. It is important that we understand how, why and by whom policy decisions are made. This enables us to judge the reasons behind their introduction. It also helps to effect change (where appropriate) or ascertain whether a policy has been effective or has created a different problem or set of problems.

Example: in his Budget speech on 2 July 1997, Gordon Brown, the Chancellor of the Exchequer, made the following statement:

> A generation of parents have waited for their government to introduce a National Childcare Strategy. From this Budget forward, childcare will no longer be seen as an after thought or a fringe element of social policy, but as an integral part of our economic policy.

What this quote demonstrates is not just a change in attitude towards childcare but the will to develop and implement 'new' social policy. In the past, the government has viewed the family as a private institution, one in which decisions about the care of children should not be interfered with (except, of course, in cases of abuse). Traditionally, it has not financed the provision of childcare or involved itself in the training of staff. However, through the registration and inspection process undertaken by Social Services, it has monitored and regulated providers of childcare services. The words of Gordon Brown, for the first time, link childcare with the economy and the labour market. The National Childcare Strategy, the Out of School Initiative and Sure Start are the means by which social policies that focus on employment, social inclusion and raising standards can be implemented. This is an economic and political response that requires cross-ministerial consultation and co-operation in order to be developed and implemented effectively.

2 SOCIAL POLICY IS CONCERNED WITH ISSUES THAT ARE SOCIAL

The very nature of social policy is such that it affects people, and it is people who make up society. The study of social policy helps us to understand how a society responds to a perceived problem or given issue. It shows us how these responses can change over time, and what appears to be important to a society at any given point in its history.

Example: Michael Oliver, in his book *Understanding Disability from Theory to Practice* (1996), reflects on his growing political awareness, the influence this had on his career development and his growing involvement with disabled people. Michael himself has a disability and has become increasingly involved in the struggle to put disability issues on the political agenda. Whilst the 1970s saw legislation developed to protect women and ethnic minorities from discrimination, people with disabilities have had to wait until the 1990s for similar recognition. This has largely been due to the historical way in which disability has been seen. It has traditionally been treated as an individual

and/or medical problem rather than as a social issue. Increasingly, disabled people have asserted their right to be treated with equal regard. Many argue that it is not the disability that disadvantages a person but society's failure to provide the means by which that person can fully participate in society.

3 SOCIAL POLICY IS ABOUT WELFARE

The term **'welfare'** is generally take to mean 'well-being'. Social policy is concerned with the well-being of society, but most often targets those who lack well-being, ie people with particular needs or problems – eg lone parents and the unemployed.

Example: Welfare to Work is a new government initiative that enables the young unemployed and single parents to train for/find employment.

activity

In small groups, find out as much as you can about the Welfare to Work scheme.

- Who is it for, what does it involve and what sort of service does it provide?
- What are the benefits and disadvantages of the scheme for:

a young people?
b single parents?

Discuss your ideas about the Welfare to Work scheme in class.

What has social policy got to do with our lives?

Social policy affects you and me and every member of society. It is difficult to see how anything is not in some way linked to

social policy. All kinds of issues affect our daily lives, such as maintaining our health and fitness – see Figure 1.1.

	Relationships	Processes	Problem areas	Institutions
Sociology				
Shared interests	Gender	Socialisation	Deviance	Family
Distinct interests	*Culture*	*Social action*	*Industrial relations*	*Religious worship*
Economics				
Shared interests	Labour market	Recession	Economic inequality	Public spending
Distinct interests	*Money market*	*Trade*	*The firm*	*Banks and finance houses*
Politics				
Shared interests	Power	Legislation	Race relations	Government
Distinct interests	*Political change*	*Voting*	*International relations*	*Party structures*
Psychology				
Shared interests	Social psychology (eg altruism, obedience)	Child development	Attitude change	Psychiatry
Distinct interests	*Crowd behaviour*	*Mentation*	*Perception*	
Social work				
Shared interests	Worker–client relations	Community care	Child abuse	Personal social services
Distinct interests	*Family functioning*	*Counselling*	*Group interaction*	

Source: Spiker, 1995.

Table 1.1 Social policy and the social sciences

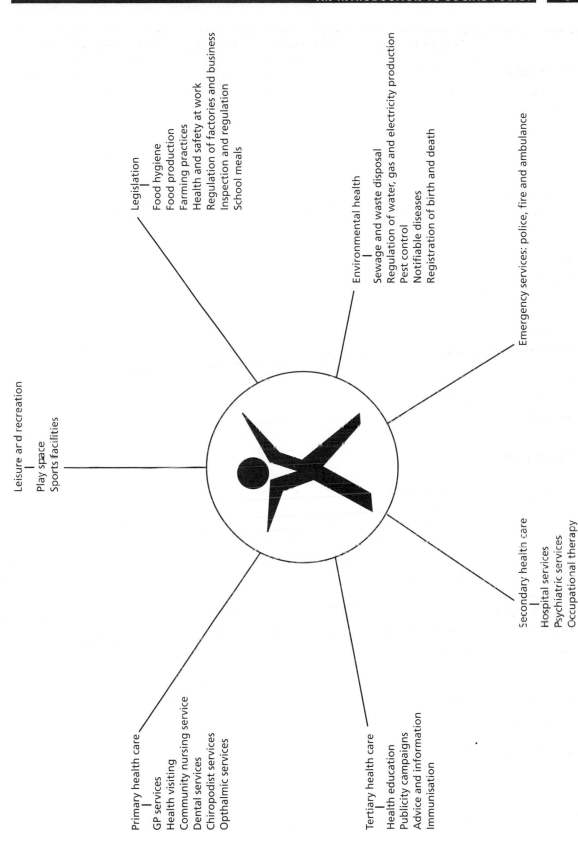

Legislation
Food hygiene
Food production
Farming practices
Health and safety at work
Regulation of factories and business
Inspection and regulation
School meals

Environmental health
Sewage and waste disposal
Regulation of water, gas and electricity production
Pest control
Notifiable diseases
Registration of birth and death

Emergency services: police, fire and ambulance

Leisure and recreation
Play space
Sports facilities

Primary health care
GP services
Health visiting
Community nursing service
Dental services
Chiropodist services
Opthalmic services

Tertiary health care
Health education
Publicity campaigns
Advice and information
Immunisation

Secondary health care
Hospital services
Psychiatric services
Occupational therapy
Screening

Figure 1.1   Spidergram: health and fitness

activity

Ideologies

An **ideology** is a set of ideas, attitudes and opinions which together form the basis of a belief system or philosophy. The word 'ideology' is commonly used to describe political ideas. Each political party is described as having a particular ideology.

POLITICAL IDEOLOGIES

The terms 'Right', 'Left' and 'Centre' are used to identify the ideology of a specific political party. Different parties can be described as 'Rightwing' or 'Leftwing' as each term covers a broad range of similar ideas. Some political ideologies may be said to be on the extreme right, such as fascism, or on the extreme left, such as Marxism. (See Table 1.2.)

Ideologies of welfare are sets of ideas that describe a society's beliefs and opinions about, and attitude towards, its personal and social services. (See Table 1.3.)

Types of social policy

The type of social policy adopted by a society will have a strong influence on that society's structure, the life chances of its citizens and the way in which that society chooses to regulate and allocate its resources. First, a society must decide what level of state intervention it finds politically, financially and socially acceptable. Second, it will develop a policy that reflects a particular model of welfare provision. Third, an eligibility or needs criterion is established for those who will benefit from the policy. Let us look in detail at the first two of these.

STATE INTERVENTION

This relates to the amount of government responsibility taken for the funding and delivery of services in the welfare state. Not all societies have the same level of intervention.

The USA has limited state intervention. The government here takes little responsibility for welfare services. It relies on the **private and voluntary sectors** to provide welfare services. State welfare is only offered to those in extreme need. Americans are expected to take out insurance to cover unforeseen medical and social circumstances.

The state in Sweden takes full responsibility for its citizens by providing a system of social welfare that attempts to ensure equality.

The British welfare state provides a national minimum to those in need but also funds and regulates services such as health, education and the social services. It has what is called a **mixed economy of welfare**. The government here takes responsibility for some things but also encourages private and voluntary intervention.

MODELS OF WELFARE

Simply, the term '**model**' means something worthy of imitation. Models represent a framework upon which to build ideas. Many of the following **models of welfare** are based on ideas originated by R. M. Titmuss.

- *Residual and selective models of welfare:* these hold that the state should provide welfare if the individual, family or private sector are unable to do so. The state applies a 'safety net' for those most in need.
- *The institutional model of welfare:* this holds that welfare provision is an important function of society. It aims to ensure a decent standard of living for all its citizens. However, it does not aim to create an equal society or to provide all services itself. This model describes a mixed economy of welfare.

Figure 1.2 Residual and selective models of welfare

Figure 1.3 The institutional model of welfare

- *The universal model of welfare:* this holds that welfare services should be made available to people as a right. Society is responsible for the welfare of all its citizens regardless of their circumstances.
- *Individual and industrial achievement models of welfare:* these hold that social welfare is part of the economy and should reward merit, performance, productivity and effort. Those who achieve and put more into society should get more out.

Figure 1.4   The universal model of welfare

Figure 1.5   Individual and industrial achievement models of welfare

Political ideology	Position	Party	Beliefs and values	Country
Conservative	Rightwing	Conservative	Family values Market economy Law and order Residual welfare	Britain
Conservative	Rightwing	Christian Democrat	Family values Religious values Market economy Residual welfare	Germany
Conservative	Rightwing	Republican	Family values Religious values Market economy Residual welfare	America
Liberal	Centre	Liberal Democrats	Family values Proportional representation Mixed economy of welfare	Britain
Liberal	Centre	Social Democrats	Family and religious values Market economy Reducing inequality	America France Spain
Marxist	Extreme Leftwing	Communist	Statism/equality Universal welfare	China Eastern Europe
Nationalist	Centre/Left	Plaid Cymru	Upholding nation state Institutional welfare Equal opportunities	Wales
Nationalist	Leftwing	Scottish Nationalists	National government Institutional welfare Equal opportunities	Scotland
Nationalist	Leftwing	Sinn Féin	National independence Institutional welfare	Northern Ireland
Socialist	Leftwing	Labour	Family values Equal opportunities Consultation Mixed economy of welfare	Britain

Table 1.2 Political ideologies

Ideology	Core values	View of society	Role of government
Anti-collective Politics: Conservative	Individualism, freedom-liberty, capitalism, efficiency and a competitive marketplace.	Believe that the family is of paramount importance in maintaining the balance of society. Emphasise self-help and a key role for the voluntary and private sector in service delivery.	Residual and selective models of welfare adopted. Minimal intervention. 'Safety net' principle of welfare provision.
Reluctant collectivists Politics: New Labour and the Liberal Democrats	Individualism, self-help, private enterprise and a mixed economy of welfare.	Concerned with the well-being of society and reducing inequality.	Residual and selective models of welfare adopted with provision for state intervention to promote social change.
Collectivist (1) Politics: socialism and Old Labour	Equality, freedom, fellowship, democracy and humanitarianism.	Society is seen as divided by social class (wealth and status).	Institutional model of welfare to promote purposeful action in order to modify injustice and social inequality.
Collectivist (2) Politics: communism	Transformation of society to one where all people are equal.	Society is seen as exploited by landowners and big business due to the inequalities of status.	Institutional model of welfare that redistributes wealth and resources. Government regulation of welfare services.
Collectivist (3) Politics: feminism	Equality and a redistribution of power between men and women.	Patriarchal: male dominance.	Action to modify inequality and discrimination on the grounds of sex. Institutional model of welfare.

Ideology	Core values	View of society	Role of government
Collectivist (4)	Equality and a redistribution of power amongst cultures and races.	Racism: white dominance.	Action to modify inequality and and discrimination on the grounds of race. Institutional model of welfare.
Politics: racist critique			

Source: Lovell and Yeo, 1998.

Table 1.3   Ideologies of welfare

Developing social policy

The development of social policy reflects the ideology of welfare adopted by the state on behalf of its citizens. Banting (1979) outlined five stages in policy-making:

1 awareness of the problem
2 the degree of importance attached to the problem
3 the definition of the problem
4 consideration of the alternatives
5 choice between the alternatives.

Social problems, or a failure in the effectiveness of policy, often precipitate change.

This might be far-reaching or just cosmetic. It might involve new legislation or the introduction of new guidelines. Banting's theory suggests that change only occurs if a problem/issue or situation of some kind is acknowledged, and that who recognises the problem and the importance they attach to it will determine how it is defined. Before making a response, policy-makers will look at various courses of action and weigh up their advantages and disadvantages. Eventually, a decision will be made about how to address the problem, issue or situation.

CASE STUDY

Juvenile crime

Juvenile crime has been seen as a social problem for generations. However, the particular concerns in the 1990s have been the age at which offending begins, the increasing number of crimes of violence, and of young women involved. These problems provoke an angry response from the public and the media. The police, the courts and juvenile justice workers, eg probation officers, are seen as 'soft on crime'. Society has defined the problem by the way that offenders are punished. The

contd. ⅠⅠⅠ➡

problem is individualised, or blame is placed on lax parenting, drug and alcohol misuse and unemployment. Successive governments have stated their intent to be 'tough on crime'. Initiatives to crack down on juvenile crime have included:

- the promotion of family life:
  - the promotion of 'good parenting'
  - monies being made available for parenting classes
  - the introduction of 'parenting classes' in schools
- controlling situations that provoke crime:
  - clamping down on drugs
  - local initiatives banning alcohol in public places
  - tighter controls on the way alcohol consumption is advertised
  - introducing drug tsars
- promoting employment:
  - Welfare to Work
  - modern apprenticeships
  - national traineeships

Such a complex social problem has demanded a range of alternatives; some such as boot camps (military-style reform institutions) were dismissed. Policy choices on the part of different governments have appeared to be an attempt to deal with the underlying causes of crime not just the crime itself.

Implementing social policy

Once a policy has been developed, it has to be put into practice by social administrators, who include:

- government ministries or departments
- county councils
- local and unitary authorities
- metropolitan borough councils
- service providers, eg hospitals and schools.

It must be remembered that Britain comprises four separate countries: England, Scotland, Northern Ireland and Wales. The way services are administered, and by whom, will differ, particularly in Scotland and Northern Ireland. These countries have their own ministries and departments, eg the Scottish Office.

Issues affecting the development of social policy

SOCIAL PROBLEMS

A dictionary would suggest that the term 'problem' means:

- a question requiring a solution
- a situation or person that is difficult to deal with or understand
- a source of distress

- a situation that requires something to be done
- an arrangement that requires a certain result to be attained
- being in trouble.

A **social problem** contains elements of all the above. A problem becomes a social one when it affects the whole or part of society. Social problems present issues for which some kind of solution is necessary. Sometimes, problems are not acknowledged. For instance, child sexual abuse was not considered an issue until the 1980s: before then, it was thought to be a very rare occurrence, too rare to be considered a social problem. The Childline service and an increasing number of disclosures have meant a rethinking of our understanding of this issue. In order for policy-makers to decide on the best response or solution to a problem, they need to know how that problem came about, what has influenced the perpetrators and the effect the abuse has on their victims. Paul Spiker (1995) suggests that responses to social problems can be classified in two ways:

1 *direct responses:* these responses address problems associated with a particular set of people or social group. The Sex Discrimination Act 1976 and European Equal Treatment Directive tackled head on the problem of social and occupational divisions made on the basis of sex. It particularly influenced the working life of women. Other direct responses tackle the underlying cause of a problem. The National Childcare Strategy (1998) attempts to address the problems experienced by working parents.

2 *indirect responses:* the health of the nation is an overarching concern of government. No one policy is able to address the health issues affecting a society. Being healthy involves too many areas of our life, as we have already seen. Policies related to leisure are just as important to our health as policies concerning the NHS. For this reason, a range of policy initiatives are necessary, anything from regulating the sale of beef to government health warnings on cigarette packets.

NEED

One of the things policy-makers will consider is what social need is being met by the development of a particular policy. Understanding the concept of 'need' is extremely important to understanding the way a society decides upon the level of intervention it finds comfortable. The idea of 'need' is complicated. We all believe ourselves to have needs. Some we recognise as more important than others. For instance, if our basic need for water, food and shelter is not met, we would eventually die. When our car breaks down for the hundredth time, on the other hand, we might feel we 'need' a new one, but the consequences here are not fatal if we cannot afford one. Social policy addresses those needs that society decides are important. In Britain, the social-security system attempts to ensure that people have enough money to meet their basic need for shelter, warmth and food. It does not, however, provide the means for you to repair your car. Health and education, on the other hand, are deemed too important to leave to the private and voluntary sectors.

The state believes it has a responsibility to address the needs of its citizens in both these areas. However, it cannot provide for absolutely every individual need in either system as this would be too costly. Getting a face-lift on the NHS, or a funded place at the football school of excellence, might prove very difficult. The state, on behalf of society, determines those needs it has a responsibility to meet and those it does not.

activity

List your own needs under the following headings:

- things you require to keep you alive
- things you require to keep in good health
- things you require to keep you emotionally stable
- things you require to make you happy.

Categorise these requirements into those provided by the state, those provided by private organisations, those provided by your family, and those provided by yourself.

ELIGIBILITY

Once a society has decided upon those needs it will attempt to meet, it has to adopt social policies that can address them. These policies will give guidance about the service and how it will be administered and delivered. Those with the responsibility for service delivery will have to decide who is actually in need and meets the criterion dictated by the policy. In order to do this, *eligibility* has to be established – see Table 1.4.

Influences on social policy

LEGISLATION

Legislation (ie the law) often dictates or informs social policy. Legislation usually contains three types of regulation:

1 *mandatory* (which *must* be done)
2 *permissive* (which *should* be done)
3 *guidance* (which concerns how something *could/should be* done).

In the case of **mandatory regulations**, all (state-controlled) agencies must follow uniform measures. **Permissive regulations** and **guidance regulations**, however, allow for local variations in both service delivery and resource allocation.

POLITICS

The ideology of the different political parties will impact on the policy-making process, with the government, ie the party in power, having the most influence here. Individual politicians can also be influential. Some politicians are more prominent than others, often speaking in the House of Commons, on radio, on TV or in the newspaper. Their views will be widely circulated and will gain them a public following that puts pressure on the government to listen to them. Individual MPs represent their own constituencies, and have a duty to put forward the public view, again influencing the policy-making process. Some MPs bring *private member's*

Question	Consideration
• What is the unit of need?	Individual, child, family, group or society
• What is the cause of the need?	Poverty, unemployment, disability or abuse
• Who is assessing the need?	Individual, professional, expert
• What problems arise because of the need?	Poverty, homelessness, crime
• What resources are necessary to address the need?	Funding, services, specialists
• What resources are available to address the need?	Money, people, buildings
• What would happen if the need were not addressed?	Crime, violence, poverty, ill health
• What agency or organisation could best meet this need?	Family, education, health, housing, social services
• Whose life chances are affected, and how?	Individual, group or society
• Is it in the interests of society to meet this need?	Yes, no, sometimes, never

Source: Lovell and Yeo, 1998.

Table 1.4 Eligibility criteria

bills. These are discussed in the House of Commons, and decisions are made about their content and whether or not they should become law. Examples of these would include the attempted abolition of blood sports and decreasing the age of consent to 16 years for homosexuals.

ADMINISTRATORS

Those with a responsibility for service delivery are in a good position to influence the policy-making process. These people might include teachers, doctors, social workers and the police, who are all able to report their findings to managers at a local level. Managers in turn relay this information to the county councillors, who can then pass the information on to the

Figure 1.6 Influences on social planning

House of Commons via their political party or MPs. All agencies involved in service delivery are involved with a government ministry, for example the Department of Education and Employment (DfEE), the Department of Health (DoH) and the Department of Social Security (DSS). Local findings eventually find their way back to ministers and government via this route. Increasingly, the private and voluntary sectors are becoming involved in the delivery of services, and are therefore increasingly influential in the decision-making process. Some private companies and voluntary organisations have a high profile, often being chaired or championed by people with influence in government and ministry circles. Princess Diana's involvement with a charity involved in the removal of landmines increased media attention on

this issue and hence drew government attention to the issue also.

THE MEDIA

The way the media choose to report an issue might well put pressure on the legislators and/or administrators to review current practice. An example of this would be the case of Louise Woodward, a young British girl who took a nannying job in America. She was accused of deliberately shaking baby Matthew Ipan to death. The trial was a long affair, reported on both sides of the Atlantic. Opinion varied, with Louise at one time being portrayed as a young innocent girl and at another as an evil child-abuser. Much was made of the unregulated nature of nannying. Since then, adverts have appeared in the British press

Figure 1.6   *continued*

Figure 1.6   *continued*

advertising surveillance equipment, and the government has attempted to address the issue by introducing an optional registration scheme (mandatory for nannying agencies). The power of the media can be a force to change attitudes and the law.

THE EUROPEAN UNION

A **directive** is an instruction handed down by the **European Parliament** in Brussels to the Member States of the **European Union** (**EU**). Some of these Directives may

activity

- *Week 1*: read one of the broadsheet newspapers such as *The Guardian* or *The Times* over the period of a week. Note down those stories that you think relate to social policy. How are these stories reported? What language is being used? Are any visual images being used? Is the story factual and objective, or anecdotal and subjective, or both? How might these stories influence public opinion?

- *Week 2*: read one of the tabloid newspapers such as *The Sun* or *The Mirror* over a week. Undertake the same task as above.
- *Week 3*: watch the evening news on TV, or listen to it on the radio. Undertake the same task as above.
- *Week 4*: compare your notes for the three weeks. What have you discovered about the way different media types cover issues related to social policy?

conflict with established policy. If this is the case, the government is usually given a period of time in which to make changes, for example for cleaning up the coastline. In some cases, the Member State can 'opt out' altogether and not adopt the Directive, or only adopt part of it, as Britain did with the **Social Chapter**. The **European Social Fund** (**ESF**) provides funding for a wide variety of projects from road-building to training. Increasingly, this funding is being used to support projects that were once funded by the state.

THE GENERAL PUBLIC

Every one of us can exert influence on the policy-making process. Once we are 18 years old, we can use our vote. We can write or talk to our MP or become involved in a campaign group (See Figure 1.7).

TECHNOLOGY

As advances are made in technology, so the way services are organised and delivered also changes. This may have an indirect influence on the way a society chooses to offer a service. For instance, some general practitioners (GPs) keep patient records on a database, dispensing with the need to keep paper records. In addition, computer-assisted diagnosis is becoming more common. Or there may be a direct effect: as technology improves, it can reduce the need for person power, leading to unemployment or changes in the nature of employment. Both these situations may require policy to address the impact on society.

CHARISMATIC FIGURES

Throughout history, individuals have emerged who have had a profound effect on the attitudes and thinking of society. They are often instrumental in the development of social policy. Examples include:

Figure 1.6   *continued*

- *Edwin Chadwick* was the first man of his era to consider the relationship between poverty and disease. His report on *The Sanitary Condition of the Labouring Population of Great Britain* (1842) was responsible for the development of sewage and waste disposal systems and clean water supplies.
- *Joseph Rowntree* undertook a great deal of research into the lives of the poor living in York and London. His reports were instrumental in bringing the plight of the poor to the middle classes and the government.
- *John Bowlby* has had an important influence on the child-rearing practices of the majority of the British public since the 1950s. He demonstrated a link between maternal deprivation (ie lack of bonding with a mother) and delinquency. His findings have since been modified, but remain influential in the field of child psychology and child development.

Figure 1.7 Examples of campaign clippings on the environment

Source: *Rambling Today*, No. 29, 1998. *Earthmatters*, No. 36, 1997.

- *Margaret Thatcher* was Prime Minister of Great Britain from 1979 until 1990. During that time, she is said to have changed the 'hearts and minds' of the British public, undermining public attitudes on health, education, housing and income maintenance, replacing a culture of dependency on the state to provide services with one of 'self-help' and 'community care'.

One figure who cannot be overlooked in the study of social policy is *Richard Titmuss* (1907–1973). Titmuss is often called the founding father of social administration, having written and lectured on all aspects of social policy and its implementation.

activity

Research the work of John Bowlby. How did his work influence the lives of parents and children in the 1950s and 1960s? Does his work still influence our thinking?

The impact of social policy

Social policy changes as society evolves. Policies that were established at the onset of the welfare state in the 1940s reflected the social attitudes of the time. These policies would not prove useful in the new millennium, however, for society has moved on. Social policy is a dynamic process which influences:

- attitudes, beliefs and values
- practice
- the delivery of services
- the way a society perceives social problems
- life chances
- social structures
- our lifestyles
- future policy.

National and regional variations

Across Britain and Europe, there exist both national and regional variations in the development of social policy and the delivery of services. Legislation and service delivery in Scotland and Northern Ireland is very different from that in England and Wales, even though all four countries are the responsibility of one government and one parliament.

A **social worker** who has been trained in England would not be able to practise in Scotland or Northern Ireland as the law is so different. They would need additional training. The same is true the other way around. In 1988, the Labour government instituted the development of Scottish and Welsh Assemblies. This move would devolve some parliamentary powers and decision-making to these Assemblies, thus creating mini parliaments. The needs of those living in the north of England differ from those living in the south; and the needs of urban communities differ from those of rural communities. Legislation and social policy allow for regional and local variation as well as national variation.

CHAPTER 2

INVESTIGATING SOCIAL POLICY

Social research tells us about the social world we live in. It can provide knowledge for the development of social policy and measure its implementation and impact.

There are a range of different methods through which social research is carried out, but they fall into two main categories: **quantitative research** and **qualitative research**.

Quantitative research measures the research subject by amount, whilst qualitative research aims to understand the kind of subject it is. Quantitative research includes surveys and experiments. Qualitative research uses participant observation, in-depth interviews and documents to collect data. Quantitative research can be criticised for trying to explain the world simply in terms of cause and effect, whilst qualitative research can be seen as subjective and not generalisable. Qualitative and quantitative methods can be used together.

The choice of research methods will depend upon the subject being researched. Secondary sources of data, such as administrative records, letters and diaries as well as official statistics, can be used for research purposes.

Research should be considered in terms of its reliability and its validity. Ethics are also important in research. If information is gathered without the research subject knowing both the purpose of the research and the fact the they are being researched, there is an ethical problem.

Research methods can be used for evaluation. Evaluation measures the progress of the subject, which is being evaluated against its aims and objectives.

Social research is often used to inform social policy. Understanding social-research methods helps us to take a critical view of the research and of how it is used.

The aim of **social research** is to tell us more about the social world we live in. Social research can:

- provide knowledge which results in the development of social policy
- measure the implementation of social policy
- measure the impact of social policy.

Social-policy research is often called *applied social research*. Such research is not, however, a requirement for the development of social policy; indeed, some social-research findings have been ignored if they do not fit in with the politics of the policy-makers.

The history of social research

The study of sociology began in Europe as a result of the significant changes in social structures, changes which arose from the process of industrialisation. Research was needed to understand the social changes that were taking place, and how best to manage these through the introduction of social policies.

In Britain, social research began in the nineteenth century. Many of the first social researchers were rich individuals with means, such as Seebohm Rowntree and Charles Booth who both conducted research into poverty in York and London respectively between 1880 and 1990. Government interest in social research, as a guide to social policy, did not start in earnest until the Second World War when the Government Statistical Service was established in 1946. From this time onwards too, universities, led by the London School of Economics, became established centres for social research. Now, social research is carried out by businesses for marketing purposes, by charities and by independent research bodies such as the Policy Studies Institute, as well as by the government and universities. In addition, a range of bodies monitor and audit the effectiveness of agencies which carry out policy in terms of **accountability** and value for money. The National Audit Office performs this function for national government, the Audit Commission for local government, and the Social Services Inspectorate for Social Services.

1801	The first Census
1837	General Register Office (for registration of deaths) established
1895	London School of Economics established, the first university centre for social research
1941	Government Social Survey established (now the Office for Population and Census Statistics or OPCS)
1946	Government Statistical Service established
1950s	Family Expenditure Survey began
1971	General Household Survey began
1973	Labour Force Survey began
1983	British Social Attitudes Survey began

Table 2.1 Historical milestones in the development of social research in Britain

activity

Find out the admissions policy of your college course, or the recruitment and selection policy of your employer.

- Who makes sure that the policy is carried out?
- Is this checked by any external agency?
- Does this change the policy in any way?

Methods of social research

As we have already noted, there is a significant relationship between social research and social policy, and any study of social policy needs to include an exploration of social-research methods in order to judge the validity of the research used. As the next section will show, there is considerable debate about, and criticism of, research methods.

There are a range of methods through which social research is carried out in order to produce information or data, and to use data to develop or test theories. Broadly speaking, these methods fall into two main categories: quantitative and qualitative; although, as will become clear, these two categories overlap and there are many different approaches in each. Particular schools of thought and perspectives inform each category.

Briefly, **quantitative research** aims to measure the subject being researched by amount, whilst **qualitative research** aims to understand the kind of subject it is.

QUANTITATIVE SCHOOLS AND METHODS

Positivism

In the early days of social research, sociologists adopted methods from science, which appeared to be able to produce objective (independent) knowledge. This school was known as **positivism**, and it concerned itself with the objective collection of social 'facts'. Auguste Comte (1798–1857) was the first person to use the term 'positive philosophy'. The results from research which uses this method are said to produce 'laws' of human behaviour, which can be generalised to the whole population.

Empiricism

Empiricism is equally influential in quantitative methods. This school shares with positivism the idea that there are 'facts' which can be gathered about the social world through neutral measures (not taking any particular view either way) in the same way as, say, sound or distance can be measured. It is described by Bulmer (1982) as 'involving the production of accurate data – meticulous, precise, generalisable – in which the data themselves constitute an end for the research'. It differs from positivism in that positivists are looking for data which will test the accuracy of a theory, whilst empiricists do not articulate a theory in their data collection.

The following are examples of quantitative methods.

Survey research

Most people will have been approached by a researcher with a clipboard in a shopping centre, wanting to find out, say, what kind of washing powder they use. This usually takes the form of **market research**, and the researcher here is using a **survey** method to test the actual or potential success of a product.

Steven Ackroyd and John Hughes (1983) describe surveys under three headings: **factual, attitudinal** and **explanatory**.

1 *Factual surveys.* These were one of the first types of survey to be used in the UK, and they aim to describe the characteristics of a population. An obvious example of this type of survey is a **census**, which covers the whole of a population. Rowntree's study of poverty in York, in which he used interviewers to go and talk to families in

their own homes, is another example of a factual survey.

2 *Attitudinal surveys.* These surveys aim to discover what people think about life in general or about specific issues in particular. An example of this type of survey is the **opinion poll**. In terms of social-policy development, particularly in a democratic society, opinion polls can be very influential. Political opinion polls aim to predict how people will vote. They assume, however, that people will do what they say they are going to do. On average, taking all the opinion polls into account, political opinion polls are fairly accurate. However, this was not the case in the General Election of 1992 when the opinion polls predicted a victory for the Labour Party and the Conservatives were voted into government!

3 *Explanatory surveys.* These types of survey are designed to test theories. Most surveys, in fact, are in some way explanatory. One example of an explanatory survey is Durkheim's study of suicide (1897). He used statistical records of suicide rates in different countries in Europe to demonstrate that there were sociological as well as psychological reasons for suicide, and was able to establish *correlations* (ie significant relationships) between suicides and other social facts.

activity

Go to your local library and look in the reference section for publications of statistics. Some examples are:

- *Social Trends*
- *Regional Trends*
- *Annual Abstract of Statistics*
- *Mortality Statistics.*

Sampling

A census collects data from the whole population to discover its characteristics, but in most cases, resources are not available to carry out a survey of this magnitude. Instead, researchers use a **sample** of the target population and then generalise the results. The advantages of using a sample are that fewer people are needed to collect and analyse the data, the accuracy of the data can be checked more easily, and the interviewers are more highly trained (Moser and Kalton, 1993).

Selecting a sample

Clearly, in order for results to be credible or valid, and generalisable to the whole population, the sample selected must be representative of the whole population.

Here the population may not refer to the whole population of the UK, but could be any group, for example schools or small and medium-sized businesses, depending on the nature of the research. The population in this sense means groups of units of analysis. A **unit of analysis** means the subject being studied. In a study of schools, the school is the unit of analysis, but in a study of people with diabetes, the individual person would be the unit of analysis.

Once the researcher has determined the total population and the individual unit of analysis, they need to create a **sampling frame**. This is the group which is somehow representative of the whole population from which the data will be collected. There are a range of sampling techniques which are used in survey research methods. The following are examples of **probability sampling methods**. These can be mathematically tested using statistical theory because, in these examples, there is a known probability of selection.

- *Simple random sampling.* Using this method, the simple rule is that each unit must have an equal chance of being selected: the researcher could put the names in a hat and draw out the number they wish to interview.
- *Systematic sampling.* When the researcher knows the size of the population and decides to interview say, 25 per cent of the population, they could take one name from every four, starting from a random point.
- *Stratified random sampling.* The first two ways of making up a sample may not ensure a representative sample of a particular group of people. For example, using a telephone directory to make up a sample would exclude people who do not have a telephone, and as, very often, it is the male adult in the household who is listed, the sample may not include enough women. Stratified sampling identifies a group by certain characteristics (age, gender, ethnicity), and thus ensures an appropriate sample from each group.

The next two examples are of **non-probability** or **purposive sampling methods** which cannot be tested under statistical theory because there is here an unknown probability of selection.

- *Cluster or multi-stage sampling.* This is a useful technique for sampling a dispersed population. Say you wanted to undertake research with health-and-social-care students all over the UK, and you wanted a sample of 1,000, you could choose a sample of further-education colleges, and then a further sample of students from each college. You would need to decide how many students could be considered from each college and how many colleges would be in the sample: this could range from 500 colleges with 2 students each to 100 colleges with 10 students each. You might need to ensure that your sample of colleges include those in urban as well as rural areas, and representation from Northern Ireland, Scotland and Wales.

- *Quota sampling.* This is often used by market researchers who are trying to represent population characteristics by dividing the population into categories of, say, gender, housing, disability, age and race. They use data from the UK Census to determine the distribution, and interviewers then have a quota target to interview. For example, if the ethnic-minority population in the area were 5 per cent, the researcher would need to ensure that 5 per cent of the people interviewed are from an ethnic-minority background.

Types of surveys

There are a variety of types of survey:

- *longitudinal surveys:* these use a sample of people which is followed over a period of time. They can provide extremely useful and valid information about social change, but they are expensive to run. An example of a longitudinal survey is the National Child Development Study which has followed a sample of children born in the first week of March 1958 throughout their lives. This study has provided information about a range of areas including infant mortality, education, parenting and employment patterns, and is often quoted by policy-makers.
- *cross-sectional surveys:* these surveys take place at one point in time. They can be regular surveys like the British Social Attitudes Survey which interviews 3,500 people from England, Scotland and Wales about their views on a range of issues on an annual basis, using different respondents each time.

- *panel surveys:* here data is collected from the same set of respondents at two or more points in time.
- *rotating sample surveys:* here, data is collected at different points in time, with some respondents replaced each time. The British Labour Force Survey, which looks at employment patterns in the British workforce, uses this method.

Some problems with surveys

Surveys often rely on the skills of the interviewer in identifying the characteristics of the respondent. For example, how does the market researcher target class when they are in the middle of a shopping centre and everyone is rushing past to do their shopping? Will there be a tendency for those people who are not in a rush to stop and answer questions? If this is so, will the results thereby be biased?

In the USA, cross-sectional surveys showed that there was very little change in the numbers and characteristics of those members of the population on welfare, and policy-makers and researchers then took these results for granted. However, other research showed that these results actually only applied to 2 per cent of people on welfare.

Low response rates (ie in return of data) are always a practical problem in survey research. A good response rate is considered to be 60 per cent, very good 70 per cent. One estimate is that 160 questionnaires have to be sent out for every 100 people in the sample.

Surveys use standard methods of data collection, asking every member of the sample the same question, and often giving a limited choice of responses such as 'Yes', 'No' or 'Don't know'. If the researcher is asking the wrong type of question because they have not understood the issue in the first place, then they may not discover the reality of the social world, which they are hoping that their research will explain. This is one of the criticisms of quantitative research.

Nevertheless, surveys provide the means to collect standardised, generalisable information about a population. They are a reliable method of collecting data, and the methods are straightforward and easy to explain (ie transparent).

activity

There has been much debate over the past few years regarding how people use their local GPs' surgeries. Some studies have pointed to the fact that many more women than men go to the doctor. Many GPs have complained that they are called out too often for insignificant illnesses.

How would you design a survey on the use of GPs in your area?

- Would the survey be factual, attitudinal, exploratory or explanatory?

- What kind of survey would you use?
- Who would your units of analysis be?
- How would you choose your sample?
- How would you maximise response?

What kind of problems might you expect? Remember:

- there may be resource considerations
- the larger the sample size, the more accurate the sample.

Questionnaires
With the exception of traffic surveys, which are usually conducted by observation, survey data is usually collected through **questionnaires**, which are either sent by post (self-completion) or else used to collect face-to-face responses (interview) or in telephone surveys.

- *Postal questionnaires.* These are a cheaper method of collecting data in comparison with a face-to-face interview, and can cover a wide geographical area more easily. Questionnaires can be easier for people to complete anonymously, which can be an advantage if you want to deal with sensitive issues such as sexual behaviour. Respondents can fill them in at a convenient time, and there is no danger that the responses could be biased by the way in which a researcher asks a question. The questions need to be straightforward and to be clear in meaning so that they can be easily understood. However, there is no control over who completes such a questionnaire: it may well be the woman rather than the man in the household, for example. It is difficult to check the bias of the sample, and also the response rate may be low.

- *Telephone surveys.* These are relatively cheap, and response rates may be high. However, respondents may break off the conversation or give short answers. Furthermore, the interviewer may bias the answers by the way in which they ask the question (this is known as *reactivity*). Telephone surveys can only be carried out with people who have a telephone, and by the person who happens to answer it! Whilst face-to-face interviews have a high response rate, they are expensive. However, the data collected here may be more extensive than with telephone surveys because the researcher can observe body language, and answers may also be more detailed, although there is still the danger of bias.

activity

List the possible advantages and disadvantages of conducting face-to-face interviews with:

- older people
- young people
- men
- ethnic minorities.

Take into account how respondents might react to you. Would they feel comfortable talking to you? What barriers might there be? Do you have any particular views about these groups of people which might bias your interpretation of what they say?

Questionnaire design

The design of questionnaires is key to the success of the research results. Table 2.2 gives some helpful hints about how to go about designing a questionnaire.

activity

Design a questionnaire on a subject of your choice. Pilot it with five people from your proposed sample, and incorporate any modifications. Evaluate what you have learnt from this process, and design some guidelines for yourself to use in the future.

Primary and secondary sources of data

Data is divided into **primary sources**: data which the researcher has collected first-hand; and **secondary sources**: data which has already been collected.

Secondary sources are wide-ranging and include administrative records, documents, letters and diaries, many of which would not have been collected for the purposes of research.

Official statistics

One of the main sources of information available to social-policy research is collected on a routine basis by the government and its agencies in the form of

Do	Don't
Explain the purpose of the questionnaire and give clear instructions.	Send out questionnaires in December.
Ask specific questions.	Use long questions or make the questionnaire too long.
Ask *closed questions* (ie involving a limited choice of answers).	Use jargon or complicated language.
Plan the questionnaire, making sure that more general questions come before specific questions.	Ask *leading questions* (ie ones where the respondent might be more inclined to answer in a particular way).
Use *filter questions*. Example: Instead of asking: *'How many cigarettes do you smoke a day?'* Ask: 1 *Do you smoke?* YES/NO 2 *If yes, how many cigarettes do you smoke per day?* Under 10 10–20 20 or over	Ask questions about money – people don't like to answer them.
Pilot (ie test out) your questionnaire.	Make your questionnaire look difficult to fill in.
Enclose a stamped addressed envelope.	Suggest that most people don't bother to respond to questionnaires.

Table 2.2 Some tips on questionnaire design

official statistics. These include the General Household Survey, the Family Expenditure Survey and the British Social Attitudes Survey. These statistics record trends within society (*Social Trends* is one of the most detailed government publica-tions on statistics). The government and social-policy-makers use official statistics to make decisions on policy issues, and to predict and measure the impact of social policies.

activity

Look at Table 2.3 showing the percentage of change in mortality rates for selected causes of death from 1951 to 1990. Note the percentage changes which have taken place between these two dates. Can you point to any changes in social policy over this period which may have contributed to these?

activity

Consider Table 2.4 showing international migration into and out of the UK. Look at the numbers of people coming into the UK (inflow) and compare this with the numbers of people leaving the UK (outflow).

- Which group of people are leaving the UK, and which group of people are coming into the country?

- Was it true that in 1980–84 this country was becoming overcrowded as a result of immigration?
- Considering UK immigration policy at the time, how do you think it relates to these statistics?

Experiments

The aim of scientific enquiry is to describe and explain in order to predict or control future events. Experiments are concerned with establishing association and causation. In experiments, in order to establish that one thing (A) has caused another thing (B), the following three conditions must be satisfied:

1 A must happen first
2 when A changes, so must B
3 all other explanations for an association between A and B must be ruled out.

These three conditions are difficult to establish anywhere other than in an experimental setting where all other variables can be ruled out. However, experiments conducted in laboratory conditions often rely on volunteers to take part, which may bias the experiment because they are not randomly selected. Volunteers may also choose to take part because of their personal interest in the process, thus creating a self-fulfilling prophecy whereby the subjects of the research *agree in advance* with the hypothesis, ie the theory being tested.

Experimental research is often used in health care, particularly for clinical trials where a new treatment is being tested. In most experimental research, a **control group** is set up, and the people in the sample are randomly allocated to either the control group or the experimental group. The control group is a group with the same characteristics as the experimental group (the group on which the

Cause of death	1951–55*	1990	% change
TB	71	4	94%
Influenza	78	7	91%
Cerebrovascular	101	57	77%
Genito-urinary	89	33	63%
Respiratory	94	58	62%
Congenital	101	56	55%
Suicide	105	72	46%
Meningococcal	96	58	40%
Heart	99	59	40%
Digestive	96	79	22%
Cancer	100	115	+15%
Skin/Musculo-skeletal	103	179	+74%

*The figures in this column are calculated by weighting the average of the age/sex specific mortality rate of the population in 1950–52. The norm is 100, and this Standard Mortality Rate (SMR) allows us to compare one death rate with another.
Source: OPCS Series DH1 no. 25 Table 25, Mortality Serial Tables, 1841–1900 England and Wales.

Table 2.3 Percentage change in mortality ratios for selected causes of death from 1951 to 1990; Standard Mortality Ratio (SMR) for 1950–52 = 100

experiment is being conducted) but is one which doesn't have the experiment conducted on it. The purpose of the control group is to enable the researcher to compare the results of the experimental group (in the case of health trials, the group which had received the drug) against a similar group of people with the same set of characteristics who had not received the drug. There is a comparison of the results before and after the trial to measure any benefits to the experimental group.

Ethical or moral issues can be involved in this type of research. For example, in the case of clinical trials or drugs to combat AIDS, activists raised fundamental questions as to whether trials were providing them with safe drugs fast enough to save lives in a health crisis. And in another quite different vein, the drug tamoxifen, which was being trialled in the prevention of breast cancer in the USA, was suspended in July 1998 because: 'the evidence suggesting that it cut a woman's risk of developing breast cancer by 45% was so compelling that continuing the trial was unethical' (Dr Richard Klausner, in Christensen, 1998).

Experiments do, however, offer a very precise measurement and hard facts about the research subject.

Criticisms of quantitative methods

Whilst quantitative methods of social research are widely used to develop social policy and to measure its impact, they are not without their critics. Underlying some of these criticisms are fundamental misgivings about positivism and empiricism and their claims to objectivity.

Country of last or next residence	Inflow (000)	Outflow (000)	Balance (000)
Commonwealth countries			
Australia	12.7	34.8	−22.1
Canada	5.7	14.4	−8.6
New Zealand	6.2	8.6	−2.4
African Commonwealth	15.0	11.8	3.2
Bangladesh, India, Sri Lanka	15.5	3.9	11.6
Pakistan	10.8	1.6	9.2
Caribbean	3.5	3.2	0.3
Other	14.6	13.8	0.8
Total Commonwealth	**84.0**	**92.1**	**−8.0**
Non-Commonwealth countries			
European Community	37.8	36.7	1.1
Rest of Europe	7.0	6.0	1.1
United States of America	20.3	28.6	−8.3
Rest of America	3.3	3.8	−0.5
Republic of South Africa	6.1	15.7	−9.6
Middle East	13.1	22.8	−9.7
Other	14.6	8.3	6.2
Total non-Commonwealth countries	**102.2**	**121.9**	**−19.7**
Total	**186.2**	**214.0**	**−27.7**
UK citizens	82.9	145.2	−62.3
Non-UK citizens	103.4	68.7	34.7

Source: Office of Population Censuses and Surveys, reproduced from *Social Trends*.

Table 2.4 Internal migration (in thousands) into and out of the UK, 1980–84

To take the philosophical perspectives first, the interpretative approach to sociology aims to interpret social action, and to understand the meanings behind it. In the social world, people construct their own meanings about reality based on their own understanding. However, this point is not taken into account in positivism, where human behaviour is simply observed and measured and conclusions are drawn without necessarily finding out about the interpretations of the subjects concerned.

Phenomenologists also believe that the social world is constructed through the meanings given to it by individuals, and reject the notion of objectivity for this reason. For researchers from these schools of thought, there is a fundamental flaw in quantitative social research which believes itself to be objective, neutral or value-free. They would argue that the researcher carries with them a range of assumptions and values which are used, even if not consciously, in the research process.

In Rowntree's research on poverty in

York, for example, which is considered to have been rigorous in its scientific approach, he used as his measure of poverty an estimate of a minimum weekly expenditure for a family of two adults and three children, and found that 28 per cent of the total population of York were living in poverty. He went on to distinguish between *primary poverty*, which was found in families whose total earnings were less than the minimum weekly expenditure, and *secondary poverty* where families, whose earnings *would* have met the minimum expenditure level, were spending additional money on useful items (furniture, clothes or a newspaper) or wasteful items (alcohol, tobacco or gambling). This definition of wasteful expenditure is a highly subjective one, based on Rowntree's and his interviewers' own moral codes.

Quantitative research has been criticised for this reason by feminists (Oakley, in the Utting Report, 1997) who have pointed out that in 80 per cent of cases, a man is defined as the head of the household and the social class of a family is defined by the occupation of the male adult. This results in a particular and sexist interpretation of the data.

A more recent example comes from official statistics which show that 10 per cent of the prison population are Afro-Caribbean, a group which only forms 1.2 per cent of the population (Home Office, 1991). This could be interpreted as demonstrating that Afro-Caribbeans are more likely to commit a crime than other groups. However, other studies have shown that discrimination is prevalent in the criminal system and that black people are more likely to be reported for an offence, stopped and searched, less likely to be cautioned rather than prosecuted, and more likely to be sentenced than other ethnic groups. The interpretation of the statistics, then, depends on the understandings and awareness of the interpreter and on the meanings which they give to the data. This is a highly subjective process.

Social researchers from these schools of thought criticise quantitative methods as being:

- *behaviourist* – ie only taking into account observations
- *reductionist* – ie only concentrating on variables
- *mono-causal* – ie explaining simply in terms of cause and effect
- artificial
- manipulative.

QUALITATIVE METHODS

Ethnography

Qualitative researchers use **ethnography**, or **field research**, as their preferred method of social research. This has been associated with the work of **anthropologists**, and starts from the assumption that people *interpret* their world and act according to their own socially-constructed meanings.

Ethnographers are committed to:

- the idea that it is how people explain the world that determines their action;
- researching everyday, naturally occurring actions (*naturalism*);
- looking at the total social context, rather than separating elements from it (*holism*);
- recognising the complexity of social processes (*multiple perspectives*).

Ethnographic methods

Researchers make use of documents, conversations, unstructured interviews and observations to collect their data. They accept that the way they ask a question may bias the way in which the respondent replies. However, rather than viewing this as a problem, they see it as a process which becomes 'normalised' and may be a basis for gaining understanding.

For example, Janet Finch, undertaking research with rector's wives, found that they talked more openly with her because she herself had been a rector's wife, and that this factor had given her more data than she would otherwise have had access to (Finch, 1993). On the other hand, this also points to an ethical problem. It may be that the researcher is deceptively empathetic with interviewees, so that they give more away about themselves than they want to.

Ethnographers adopt a variety of methods to collect data, and these are called *covert* and *overt*. Overt methods are where the researcher is open with the respondents about the nature of the research. Covert methods are used when the researcher does not want to jeopardise their access to the research area by stating their aim. For example, if a researcher wants to look at the use of marijuana amongst professional people, they might feel that they are unlikely to gain much data by explaining what they are doing.

This too poses some clear ethical problems, in that the researcher may well find themselves in a position whereby they are deceiving people about their role. The researcher needs to make ethical decisions about whether the ends, in this case, getting information about marijuana use amongst professionals, justify the means, in other words, deception.

Ethnographers use *participant observation* as a means of gathering data. Participant observation roles vary from the complete participant, where the researcher belongs to the group or organisation being researched and does not state their research intention, to the participant as observer, where the researcher tells the research subject what they are doing, to the complete observer, where the researcher is outside the group being researched.

Participant observation enables the researcher to understand better how people interpret their social world. The fact that the researcher is involved in the process is seen not as a problem but as a way of understanding by being part of the situation, and therefore as a valuable source of data in itself. This is known as *reflexivity*.

activity

Practising participant observation

Select a café, pub, restaurant or wine bar to sit in. Observe for 20–30 minutes. Record what you hear and see in as much detail and as neutrally as possible, without interpreting why people are doing what they are doing. Note the sequence of events, the frequency and any patterns you can make out, as well as groupings and non-verbal behaviour. Describe the physical setting, and concentrate on one group if necessary. Write your observations on one side of a double-sided notebook, and on the other any thoughts you may have about what is going on, so as to separate your observation from your interpretation. Note any difficulties, and whether, at any point, your act of observing affects the scene you are observing.

When you have finished, try to explain what you think has been going on from the perspective of the people you have been observing. What have you learned about the problems and possibilities of participant observation? Did you identify any aspects or themes which would be worth exploring further?

Ethnography is well-suited to research which seeks to understand human actions, and can often enable knowledge to be gained, about a social setting, which would not have been evident from large-scale survey researches or questionnaires. The researchers here are seeking to establish *subjective adequacy*, ie something which makes sense to the people being researched, rather than *causal adequacy*. One advantage that ethnography has over quantitative methods is flexibility. If, halfway through the research, it becomes obvious that one line of questioning is not working, questionnaires cannot be changed, but the ethnographer can use this new knowledge to further explore their subject.

Doing research using qualitative methods

Once the research topic has been decided on, the researcher has to decide how to collect the data. One of the first issues to address is how to gain access to the research subject. If the researcher wishes to investigate how an organisation works, they need to consider how to become part of the organisation. If the organisation does not wish to be investigated through a research project which may be critical of their practice, the researcher may have to find a covert means of access instead. The researcher needs to become an accepted part of the social scene. Sometimes, a *gate-keeper*, ie someone who acts as an intermediary between the researcher and the group, can be used. The researcher needs to consider their own acceptability to the group they are studying in terms of gender, age, ethnicity etc, whether they will be an insider or an outsider, and how this will affect the research process.

In ethnographic research, non-probability sampling methods are used, and these include purposive, theoretical and opportunistic sampling. The *snowballing* technique is also sometimes used. This is where the researcher is introduced to other potential respondents by becoming involved in the social scene. The researcher may wish to use a quota-sampling method to include the range of people represented within a particular context. The researcher here may sample people, time and place.

The researcher needs to have an orientating theory, or sensitising concepts, ideas or hunches, which guide the research process initially, and which may be modified as the research continues.

Field notes are one of the main sources of data. The researcher here logs all their observations, in terms of conversations overheard, body language, and actions and behaviour of the research subjects. These notes form the basis of material for analysis. Bruyn (1966) suggests six areas for the researcher to bear in mind when collecting data in the field:

1 *time:* the more time a researcher spends with a group, the greater the understanding;

2 *place:* the physical environment;
3 *social circumstances:* the relationships between people and their environment;
4 *language:* verbal and non-verbal forms of communication;
5 *intimacy:* access to the private world which lies behind the actions of the research subjects;
6 *social consensus:* the extent to which people share an understanding about social meanings.

Data analysis

In ethnographic research, the process of analysis takes place at the same time as that of data collection. Data is collected and sorted into potentially meaningful categories by some method of 'constant comparison' (Glaser and Strauss, 1967), and these categories are then reconsidered in the light of further data. *Triangulation*, ie testing out data collected through one method – say, interviews – against documentary evidence and participant-observation field notes, is used to confirm categories. In this way, the researcher builds up a theory as the research progresses, and constantly tests it out to theoretical saturation point, ie to the point where no further explanations occur and there appears to be consensus on the categories reached.

Qualitative methods can explain why humans act as they do in a way which quantitative methods may not. However, they depend absolutely on the ability of the researcher, and there is a danger that this individual will place their own bias when interpreting the data. In addition, qualitative research mainly takes place in small-scale settings, and it can be argued that its findings are not generalisable. It is thus seen to be low on external validity. However, it is high on ecological validity, ie in terms of giving an interpretation of social meanings which is valid for the people in the research sample.

activity

How would you go about undertaking qualitative research to study lone parents' attitudes to employment? Consider:

- which method to use: participant observation or interviewing (semi-structured or unstructured. Semi-structured interviewing is where the researcher has a list of questions or topics that they want to cover over the course of the interview and will steer the discussion along those lines. Unstructured interviewing is where the interview is free-ranging, with no particular structure imposed by the researcher);
- how to choose your sample and what you will sample;
- whether your research will be covert or overt;
- how acceptable you will be to the target group;
- how you feel about the issue yourself;
- how you will gain access to the group.

Give reasons for your choices, and note any difficulties you might face.

Testing research for validity and reliability

Research should be considered in terms of its *reliability*, ie whether research methods can be replicated with the same material, and whether the results can be checked, and in terms of its *validity*, ie whether it is a true picture of social reality. Data can be reliable without being valid. Table 2.5 shows how particular research methods measure up in terms of validity and reliability.

	Experiments	Surveys	Ethnography
Internal validity	High		
External validity	Low	High	
Reliability			Low
Ecological validity			High

Table 2.5   Assessing research validity and reliability

A CHECK LIST FOR ASSESSING RESEARCH

* Can you generalise the results to a wider population?
* How did the researcher make sure that the data was reliable?
* What steps did the researcher take to make sure that their effect on the responses of the subjects was limited?
* What claim does the author make for the results of the research?
* Can you find any of the possible explanations?

(This check list was adapted from the Open University, Block 8, Evaluation of Research, DE304, p. 18.)

Combining methods

This chapter has considered both quantitative and qualitative methods separately, but in reality, researchers often combine the two. Qualitative research often explores a particular issue, with subsequent findings then used to devise larger-scale quantitative studies. Newby, in his study of Suffolk farm workers, used his qualitative research to interpret his quantitative data (Newby, 1977). The UK Census, which did not include any questions on ethnicity until 1991, had to rely on qualitative research to define its categories.

Ethics

There are important ethical issues involved in research. We have already seen that a degree of deception takes place in qualitative research. One example of this is Humphreys' (1970) research in a public toilet regularly used for homosexual encounters. He acted as 'look-out' where he was also assumed to find sexual enjoyment in his role as 'voyeur'. He took the numberplates of men who had been involved in these encounters, and through contacts in the police, discovered that a large number were married.

There are issues about informed consent in research projects, about whether participants have the right not to participate (this has been true for education research conducted with schoolchildren) and about whether confidentiality is guaranteed. There are a range of questionable practices, which include:

- coercing people to participate
- withholding information about the nature of the research

- invasion of privacy
- not treating participants with respect
- possible harmful effects of research intervention.

Research is often undertaken with deprived groups of people, and there is a tendency to 'study down'. This refers to the fact that the subjects of research often hold little power in society. The researcher has both power and status, and there is an unequal and possibly exploitative relationship set up right from the start of the research project.

Research which is used to develop policy can be used for other purposes than that for which it was intended, and over which the researcher has no control. **Action research** is one method which minimises ethical risks. This is a collaborative effort, with research participants themselves involved in undertaking the research and acting on the findings to improve a situation.

Evaluative methods

Evaluations are conducted for a variety of purposes. *Accountability* is the particular aim of bodies like the National Audit Office or the Audit Commission. The question being asked here is whether value for money in public spending has been achieved and whether money has been spent appropriately. Public relations also drive evaluations, to enable an organisation to prove its worth. The real purpose of an evaluation is to discover

whether an organisation or a project is doing what it set out to do, and to learn from the findings to better understand what is going on and how to move forward for the future.

Evaluative methods aim to collect data from a variety of sources: interviews with all stakeholders (ie all those with an interest in the project), records and key events. Data is collated and measured against the original aims and objectives of a project.

The process of research

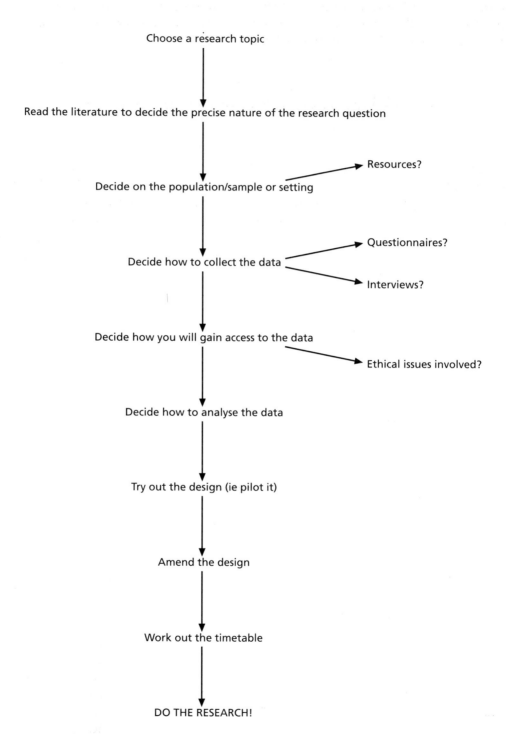

Figure 2.1   How to do your own research

Evaluations can be both **summative**, ie involving a summary of final data, and **formative**, ie providing an understanding of the processes through which a project has moved to get to its current position.

The final evaluation should inform an action plan to build on the results. Evaluations are very useful in providing data as to whether or not a policy has been achieved.

The uses of social research

Throughout this book, you will find examples of social research which have led to the development of social policy, or to a change in social policy. If you read the newspaper, listen to the radio news, or watch the news on television, you will hear examples of research quoted to back up a call for a new policy or to justify an existing policy. As a student of social policy, it is important for you to be able to take a critical view of social research and its methods in order to better understand the context in which social policies are made.

CHAPTER 3

A HISTORICAL OVERVIEW: SOCIAL CONDITIONS BEFORE 1940

Poverty was one of the first social problems in Britain that sparked a response from the government and the general public, leading to policies that were social in nature.

Many of the responses to poverty formulated as early as 1388 are still reflected in our present benefit system.

A number of influential ideas shaped the attitudes and policies established before the First World War. As the population grew, concerns were expressed about Britain's ability to provide food and homes for increasing numbers of people, and arguments were made for population control. The principle of **self-help** argued that people should do things for themselves and not rely on the state. The **utilitarian** principle held that the law should punish any action that did not promote the greatest good for the greatest number of people. The theory of *laissez-faire* maintained that industry and business should be allowed to trade freely and without government restriction.

Both agricultural reform and the Industrial Revolution had a profound impact on the way people lived and worked.

Urbanisation and a number of cholera epidemics led to Edwin Chadwick's publishing his *Report on the Sanitary Conditions of the Labouring Population of Great Britain* in 1842. The ideas expressed in his Report later found both political and public support, and were instrumental in the development of sewage and waste-disposal systems, clean water supplies and a Central Board of Health.

During the nineteenth century, the British Empire was influential around the world, creating the wealth to support policies that benefited the general public and especially the labouring classes. Until the 1900s, the state played a minor role in the development of policy. It stepped in only when absolutely necessary. In the main it was left to the Church, charities and concerned individuals to provide services for those in need. Between 1905 and 1914, however, a Liberal government instituted legislation that established a raft of social policy and gave the state a central role in ensuring that this was delivered. Lloyd George's **People's Budget** raised revenue for social reform from taxes that predominantly affected the upper and middle classes and yet positively benefited the working class.

The rise of the Labour Party (1900) and the **trade unions** gave the working class a stronger voice and greater power to influence government.

The First World War (1914–18)

prompted the government to address the living and physical conditions of the working class. Its aim was to address poverty, housing, health and education in a more strategic and comprehensive manner.

The importance of the past

We live in an era of rapid change, with technological, scientific and medical advances being made every day. It is easy to forget that our grandparents and great grandparents were born into different worlds, just as the grandchildren of the future will be. The past, the present and the future are linked. Discoveries made at one point in our history may affect the lifestyles of people in the present and serve as a springboard for ideas that will be shaped in the future. For instance, on 14 February 1946, IBM introduced an 'electronic brain' capable, it said, of calculating in seconds what it takes the human brain hours to calculate. Then in 1982, the silicon chip began to revolutionise the use of computers in both the workplace and the home. Many of the people working on the initial IBM project were dead by this time, but their impact on our lives and lifestyle is unquestionable. What has happened in the past and the way people lived their lives is especially important in understanding the development of social policy over time.

activity

Draw up a simple interview schedule that asks questions related to an area of social life or welfare service. For instance, at what age did you start and leave school? Did you go to different schools at different ages? Did you take exams? Ask people born in the following periods if you can interview them.

- 1920–30
- 1931–44
- 1945–59
- 1960–74
- 1975–85.

Compare their answers with those of your classmates in a class discussion. How have the areas of social life or the delivery of welfare services changed? What has remained the same? Were there any local differences, or differences between rural and urban communities? Remember: your answers will only give you a very general picture.

Poverty

Britain has a long history of providing poor relief. As early as the fourteenth century (1388), a labour shortage gave rise to a law which set out how the state should provide for those out of work. It tried to fix wages, and gave responsibility for the poor to local parishes, preventing people from moving from parish to parish in search of work. Laws against vagrancy or homelessness were the origins of poor relief. The restriction of mobility was in part due to the feudal nature of society then, ie where people bore allegiance to one master, and in part due to a general fear of social unrest and begging. However, the law did not stop people moving around the country in search of work, despite beatings and being put in the stocks. Begging and petty theft were also considered a social problem, and the result was the development of a more constructive approach to these problems. In 1536, parishes were authorised to collect money in order to support the sick and disabled so that they no longer needed to beg. Over time, a number of acts were passed that established the responsibility of society for those in 'genuine need'. The Poor Law of 1601, commonly known as the 43rd of Elizabeth, identified three main groups of poor people:

1 *the impotent poor:* this group comprised the aged, chronically sick, blind and mentally ill – these people were seen as poor through no fault of their own, and were accommodated in almshouses and poor houses.
2 *the able-bodied poor:* this group largely comprised the unemployed. These people were set to work, at a house of correction or a workhouse, in order to instil in them the appropriate work ethic and enable them to provide for themselves. These places often had a brutal regime. This group was often unemployed because of work shortages.
3 *the able-bodied who absconded:* these people were deemed vagrant and idle. They were 'punished' in the house of correction, and were considered unemployed by choice.

Since each parish was responsible for its own poor, it became necessary to clarify who belonged to which parish. The famous Settlement Act of 1662 established that the right to belong to a parish was conferred by birth, marriage, apprenticeship and inheritance. A stranger could be removed within 40 days.

The name for the Speenhamland System was taken from the Berkshire parish whose magistrates in 1795 introduced scales of relief for labourers based on the price of bread and the size of the labourers' families. This system introduced the first graduated rates of pay for benefit. Whilst this system is long gone, the idea of benefit rates being determined by family size or other criteria is not. Family Credit, for instance, is paid to top up low wages, and Income Support is paid at different rates according to age, a child receiving less than an adult.

From the 1600s, relief was paid in two ways:

1 *outdoor relief:* paid to those living in their own homes in the form of goods or money;
2 *indoor relief:* the provision of workhouse accommodation.

And as already mentioned, relief is now paid in the form of *benefits*.

activity

Draw up a chart that shows the benefits available to these individuals or groups of people:

- the unemployed
- children
- the disabled
- the sick
- the pregnant
- older people.

THE WORKHOUSE

A Royal Commission into the poor laws in 1834 resulted in the Poor Law Amendment Act 1834 which increased the use of the workhouse. This Act provided for maintenance in a workhouse to all those who applied for relief. The workhouse test or scheme of 'less eligibility' was imposed on all those seeking help. It attempted to distinguish between the deserving and the undeserving poor, the deserving poor being the sick, disabled, aged and unintentionally unemployed, and the undeserving poor being the feckless, idle and intentionally unemployed. Only those without means were offered help. The means-test is still used today. It is the way we work out if people are on a low enough income to obtain benefits. The workhouse and receipt of benefit were disliked: people felt belittled and had a negative image of themselves. This is still the case for some people who claim benefit today. Workhouses were usually segregated, with women and children in one and men in another. This meant that families were inevitably split up. Workhouses were renowned for their rigid regimes and strict rules. Life in the workhouse was made deliberately uncomfortable to encourage people to manage without relief. Fear of the workhouse became popular folklore.

activity

Take a large sheet of paper and divide it in half. Head one half 'Workhouse' and the other 'Bed & Breakfast Accommodation'. List the possible advantages and disadvantages of living in these environments. Compare your list. What parallels, if any, can you draw? Do you think living in Bed & Breakfast accommodation could be viewed as the workhouse of the twentieth century?

Workhouse children

Influential Idea 1: population control

The 1834 Act had been hotly contested, with many wishing to replace the Poor Law entirely. The Reverend Thomas Malthus wrote an *Essay on the Principle of Population*, published in 1798 and sold out in five editions by 1826. Malthus argued that, unless checked, population growth would outstrip the means of subsistence. In essence, the output of food available could not keep pace with a growing population. He insisted that the problem of poor relief could only be solved by bringing the growth in the population under control. He maintained that men should not marry and have children unless they had the means to support them. David Ricardo, in his *Principles of Political Economy* (1817), argued for a 'wage fund' from which relief would be paid.

Agricultural reform

During the period 1700–1850, farming practices changed beyond recognition. The main changes included a greater intensity of productive land use, the reduction of fallow and waste land, the introduction of crop rotation, and the introduction of higher yielding crops and animal breeds.

In addition, the increased levels of world trade saw cheap imports of grain, which prompted the Corn Laws of 1815. Prohibitively high duties were imposed on foreign corn to restrict its sale in the UK. The Laws were amended in 1828, and repealed in 1846. Inevitably, increased mechanisation meant fewer labourers were required to work the land, and as a result, many people were forced to look for work in the towns and cities. In response to this situation, gangs of labourers travelled the country, smashing up the new machinery that was taking away their living. The Tolpuddle Martyrs (1833) were agricultural labourers from Dorset who were organised into a trade union by Methodist preacher George Loveless (1796–1874). They were convicted of taking illegal oaths and transported. However, this action inspired large protests by fellow agricultural workers, and they were eventually pardoned. Far from the romantic ideal suggested by popular images of the time, life working the land was hard. People worked long hours and often undertook back-breaking and potentially dangerous tasks. Poverty was endemic, with people often living in tied accommodation, making them vulnerable to the whims of the farmer for whom they worked.

activity

Read *Lark Rise to Candleford* (1945) by Flora Thompson or *Cider with Rosie* by Laurie Lee, which both describe the period of change from agriculture to industrialisation.

The Highland clearances, famine and emigration

There are few issues in Scottish history that rouse such passions as the clearances. Explanations for why these occurred differ. One view holds that population growth had put pressure on the land so that human congestion led to the clearances. Another view maintains that wealthy landowners could make more money if they replaced the traditional practice of crofting with sheep farming. This reduced the need for labour and put crofters out of a job. It is said that, between 1807 and 1821, the Countess of Sutherland removed more than 700 families from their farms. Another view is that, as elsewhere in Britain, farming methods were changing and a drastic change in the pattern of settlement was taking place across the country. Agriculture was in decline and jobs were scarce. Towns and cities were growing, with jobs to be found in the factories.

The plight of the Highlanders was exacerbated by famine in the late 1840s. Three-quarters of the population of the north-west Highlands was without food in August 1846. (A similar famine had hit Ireland the year before (1845) when the potato crop failed.) Both landlords and the government were slow to provide relief. As a result of the famine, 16,000 people emigrated to North America or Australia between 1847 and 1856. (This section was adapted from Lynch, 1992.)

Influential Idea 2: self-help

Samuel Smiles's famous book *Self Help* was published in 1859. The spirit of **self-help**, he said, is the root of all genuine growth in the individual. He believed (a) that 'heaven helps those that help themselves', (b) 'that help from others (including the state) is enfeebling', and (c) 'that whatever is done for men or classes, to a certain extent takes away the stimulus and necessity of doing it for themselves'. This idea was extremely popular at the time and was revisited during the 1980s. Mrs Thatcher was a firm advocate of Smiles's work and believed that the welfare state had become the 'nanny state'. The unemployed were encouraged to travel to seek employment or to set up businesses of their own. Benefits were cut, but initiatives encouraging private enterprise and the entrepreneurial spirit flourished.

The Industrial Revolution

It is often assumed that Britain had no social policy until the welfare state came into being. We can see from the above discussion on poverty that this is not the case. Derek Fraser, in his book *The Evolution of the British Welfare State* (1985), argues that the development of the welfare state was gradual and evolutionary. He charts the history of social policy from the first UK Census taken in 1801. It is his view that the Industrial Revolution changed the way people lived, and that the result was a total transformation of social policy and of the state's view of its responsibility. For the term 'revolution' to be used, something must be turned upside down, and quickly – in this case, the way in which people worked and lived. England was the first country to experience industrialisation. This began in the 1740s and lasted into the late nineteenth century. It is argued that some countries such as India are only experiencing it now.

Influential Idea 3: utilitarianism

The ideas of Jeremy Bentham (1748–1832) dominated the period 1830–70. Bentham was interested in the law. He believed that laws should be socially useful and not merely reflect the status quo. He argued that all actions were right when they promoted 'the greatest happiness of the greatest number'. In essence, Bentham believed that the outcome was more important than the action. If a person's action adversely affected others, then it did not promote the greatest good or happiness, and thus should be punished by law.

Actions that had the opposite effect, on the other hand, should be supported by the law. Supporters of his ideas of **utilitarianism**, called Benthamites, tried to apply them to social policy. Traffic lights are a good Benthamite example. When travelling by car, we are required to stop at a red light, and not doing so could result in prosecution. Traffic lights are an essential means of promoting the greatest happiness for the greatest number because they reduce accidents.

Public health

The rise in urbanisation resulted in the growth of major cities such as Manchester, Liverpool and Birmingham. In 1801, London had a population of 800,000; by 1851, a further million could be added to this total. The population of Britain as a whole doubled at around the same period of time. The shift in population from rural to urban areas created a public health problem. It became clear that a combination of medical, administrative, civil-engineering and legal measures would be needed to combat the problem.

crowded into cellars and attics. Housing was also in close proximity to the unregulated factories. Residential developments did not provide adequate drainage, water or sewage supplies. Refuse built up, with no one responsible for its clearance. Water was often in short supply, with control in the hands of a few private stock companies that had little experience of coping with the prevalent level of demand. Central government failed to address all of these problems.

PUBLIC HYGIENE

It was not just the size of the population but also the pace of change that made finding adequate solutions so difficult. For a start, housing was scarce, with people

CHOLERA EPIDEMICS

A series of cholera epidemics between 1831 and 1867 affected not only the working-class labourers but also the middle class. In June 1831, the Central Board of Health was established, with other local boards created across the country. The Cholera Act of 1832 legislated for procedures and gave powers to the local health boards. However, 22,000 died, and over 50,000 people a year were dying of other fevers (such as yellow fever) caused by poor sanitary conditions. The increasing death toll generated interest in public health matters. A number of surveys were undertaken (John Haygarth 1744, John Heysham 1784, Charles Turner Thackrah 1831, Richard Miller and James Kay 1832), all of which concluded that disease was caused by 'filth, nastiness and overcrowding'.

AN IMPROVEMENT IN SANITARY CONDITIONS

Edwin Chadwick (1800–90) was, as mentioned earlier, the first man of his era to consider the relationship of poverty to disease. His *Report on the Sanitary Condition of the Labouring Population of Great Britain*, published in 1842, produced conclusive evidence of the link between environment and disease. Chadwick was responsible for the development of sewage and waste-disposal systems, and clean water supplies. However, it took some time for his ideas to be implemented.

(Adapted from: Derek Frazer (1985) *The Evolution of the British Welfare State*.)

The British Empire and imperialism

'Imperialism is the policy or goal of extending the power and rule of a government beyond the boundaries of its original state and taking into one political unit other nations or lands' (Robertson, 1985). The motives for creating an empire vary greatly:

- political control
- military control
- wealth creation
- exploitation of mineral and other resources
- power.

In Britain's case, one could argue that all of the above motives held true. In 1900, the Empire, stated one newspaper, 'stretching around the globe, has one heart, one head and one policy'. By 1906, the British Empire occupied one-fifth of the land surface of the globe (see Figure 3.1), and its population was estimated at 400,000,000. It had expanded rapidly, and at the time of the 1861 Census, it occupied 850 million square miles. This very large area of occupation gave Britain not only enormous wealth but also a great deal of influence over world politics.

The Empire's influence on social policy at home is hard to define. The wealth created would certainly have enabled individuals and the government to invest in policies that would benefit society generally. For instance, George Cadbury (1832–1922), in partnership with his brother Richard (1835–1899), established a model village for workers in Bournville, Birmingham which became a prototype for modern housing and town planning. This would not have been possible without the wealth and resources made available by the Empire.

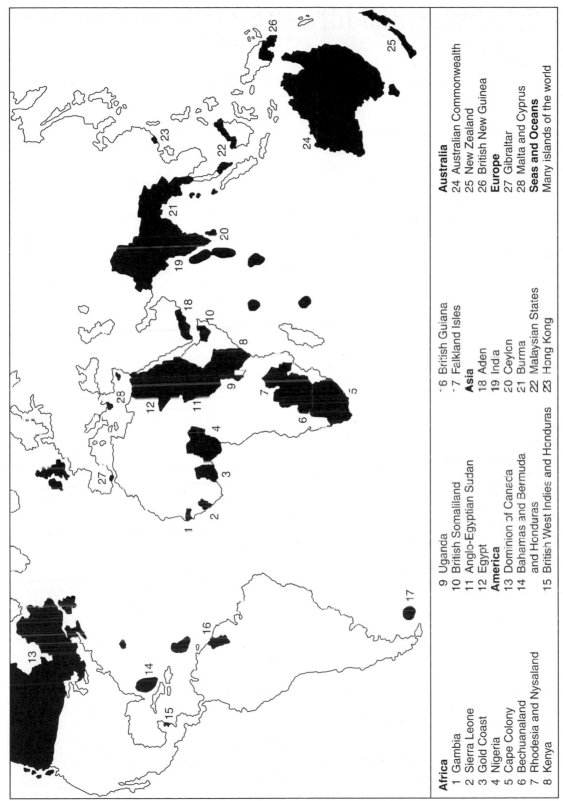

Africa
1 Gambia
2 Sierra Leone
3 Gold Coast
4 Nigeria
5 Cape Colony
6 Bechuanaland
7 Rhodesia and Nysaland
8 Kenya
9 Uganda
10 British Somaliland
11 Anglo-Egyptian Sudan
12 Egypt
America
13 Dominion of Canada
14 Bahamas and Bermuda and Honduras
15 British West Indies and Honduras
16 British Guiana
17 Falkland Isles
Asia
18 Aden
19 India
20 Ceylon
21 Burma
22 Malaysian States
23 Hong Kong
Australia
24 Australian Commonwealth
25 New Zealand
26 British New Guinea
Europe
27 Gibraltar
28 Malta and Cyprus
Seas and Oceans
Many islands of the world

Figure 3.1   The British Empire in 1906

Influential Idea 4: 'laissez-faire'

Also allied to notions of Empire was the influential Victorian idea of *'laissez-faire'* (literally 'leave alone to do'). This idea maintains that industries and businesses should be allowed to establish their trade freely and without restrictions. Quotas, regulations and prohibitions are not acceptable. The strength of this belief, however, made it difficult for the government to undertake reforms that would protect the workforce or enhance their living standards. In 1776, Adam Smith wrote:

> according to the system of natural liberty, the sovereign (state) has only three duties to attend to ... first, the duty of protecting the society from the violence and invasion of other independent societies (war); secondly, the duty of protecting as far as possible, every member of the society from injustice and oppression (crime, discrimination and abuse) ... or the duty of establishing and administering justice (law and order); and thirdly, the duty of erecting and maintaining certain public works and certain public institutions (the National Theatre and National Ballet)
> (Adam Smith, *The Wealth of Nations*, 1776 – cited in Spiker, 1995)

John Stuart Mill, in 1859, asserted that the only case for interfering in the liberty of mankind is to prevent harm to others. Herbert Spencer was an opponent of any state intervention. He bitterly criticised the government for over-legislation and over-government, as did Margaret Thatcher in the 1980s.

THE CHURCH, CHARITY AND PHILANTHROPY

Until the 1900s, the state played a minor role in the development of social policy. It stepped in only when absolutely necessary, as we saw in the sections concerned with poverty and public health. In the main, it was left to the Church, charitable organisations and individual philanthropists (ie people benevolent to fellow citizens) to provide services for the destitute, aged, sick and disabled. A key role, indeed, was played by such individuals and organisations in highlighting issues of concern. Most people attended Church, or at least believed in 'God' and the power of the Church. The belief at that time focused not on earthly happiness but on attaining happiness in heaven. Early social policy was founded on charitable principles and not, as later, on equality and the redistribution of wealth. The notion of charity was central to Victorian philanthropy. In 1861, there were approximately 640 charities. The Poor Laws were only able to address part of the public's need for help. The ideas of Samuel Smiles (ie those of self-help) were in decline, and charitable activity increased. All of the religious denominations had charities to cater for their own poor. These were usually set up in response to a particular need and were not locally or nationally organised. *Visiting societies* became popular. These were an attempt to bring the poor and the middle class into personal contact. These charities would go out and seek the needy, whilst others provided places of refuge, schools, hospitals, orphanages, reformatories and asylums. The Peabody

Trust, which is still active, provided housing. Octavia Hill and Mary Carpenter concentrated their efforts on the destitute. Mary Carpenter established 'ragged schools' (ie schools for poor children),

Octavia Hill housing settlements. The RSPCA, the YMCA, Dr Barnardo's, the Salvation Army and the RNLI were all established at this time.

---

activity

Choose one of the charities mentioned above and undertake a piece of project work. Find out as much as you can about its history, development and current philosophy. How has its work changed over time? And what projects does it have in your local area?

Education

Prior to industrialisation, the education of the working classes was not a consideration. A few 'employers' or clergy taught servants or farm workers to read and write, but these were few and far between. Education was the province of the middle and upper classes, and it had to be paid for, with boys often going away to school or having home tutors. Some families educated their female children, but few beyond reading and writing. Their education was confined to the needs of polite society and home management, and it was presided over by a governess. Industrialisation saw the formation of two distinct viewpoints about the education of the working class. Many believed that education would make the working class insolent to their 'superiors', and in addition, 'books' were seen as the cause of the French Revolution. However, some believed that education would instil the right attitudes and values and act as a form of social control. The Church took the view that education, if taught within

the Christian doctrine, would teach morality and social deference. It was the view of most that education should be not compulsory but a choice. Education for the working class thus emerged containing these three characteristics:

1 social deference
2 morality taught through a Christian ethic
3 a voluntary status.

These three planks remained in place until the mid-1900s.

In 1811, the Anglicans founded a National Society, its aim being to promote Christian knowledge by setting up schools, and similarly, the nonconformists organised their own schools through the British and Foreign Schools Society. There was rivalry between the two societies and their leading educationalists. Andrew Bell developed his system of education in India and introduced his ideas into Anglican schools (then called *parochial schools*) on his return. Joseph Lancaster, a

Quaker, had run his own school in London and had developed similar methods. Neither could agree who originated the system. Both were based on a monitorial system, with older pupils teaching younger ones.

As the cause for the education of the working class gathered momentum, the shortage of suitable buildings and teachers became apparent. It was on these grounds that the government responded. The Whig (Conservative) Viscount Althorp provided £20,000 in 1833 to spend on school buildings in the form of a grant. This sowed the seed for state intervention in education. In 1839, the government set up a Privy Council which became involved in teacher training and appointed schools inspectors. Dr James Kay, later Sir James Kay Shuttleworth, became its first secretary. Under Kay's guidance, the inspectors spread ideas, gave advice and encouraged the development of education. In 1846, W. F. Hook, a vicar of Leeds, suggested a state system of education which was not dominated by the Church. This led to a strengthening of the work of the Privy Council, which gave generous grants to schools. By the time Kay retired in 1849, the principle of state intervention in education was established, along with the administrative machinery. However, the reality was still some way off. In 1856, the Council became the Education Department. In 1858, a royal commission was set up to look at the enormous growth in this sector and it reported in 1861. It established that approximately 13 per cent of the population attended *voluntary schools* aided by the state. Most only attended for one year, and few beyond the age of 11. The education of the younger children was said to be neglected. The commission recommended:

- the extension of elementary instruction;

- reducing the many grants available to two: a central grant based on attendance and a local grant based on pupil achievement;
- concentration on 'The Three Rs': reading, writing and arithmetic.

In 1870, Gladstone's Liberal government introduced an Education Act which established the right of every child to receive some form of schooling. This came at a time when more of the working class were given the vote via the Reform Act of 1867. Following this, Robert Lowe, Vice President of the Education Department, said, 'I believe it will be absolutely necessary to compel our future masters to learn their letters', strengthening again the case for state-run education. In 1869, the National Education League was founded. W. E. Forster undertook pilot surveys of four principal cities and found less than 10 per cent of the child population in school. As a result, *board schools* were established in areas of educational need. These were intended to supplement the voluntary schools, not replace them. By 1900, 54 per cent of the elementary-school population was in board schools. Some areas began to make school compulsory. In 1876, what became known as the Sandon Education Act set up school attendance committees and placed the responsibility for attendance on parents. The Mundella's Education Act of 1880 made attendance compulsory for children aged between five and ten. Fees were about 3d (old pence) a week, but were waived for 'needy' children. The Cross Commission reported, in 1888, on the use of public money in schools, and the 1890 code abolished grants for attainment, enabling a widening of the curriculum. In 1902, the Balfour Education Act legalised secondary and technical schools by abolishing school boards and giving control to local authorities.

Social policy 1905–14

In December 1905, Arthur James Balfour resigned as the Conservative Prime Minister. He was replaced by the Scottish Liberal Sir Henry Campbell-Bannerman. The incoming Liberal government was seen as weak and fragmented. However, Bannerman established firm leadership. An election was held in 1906, and this gave the Liberals a landslide victory. Bannerman lost his seat, and Lord Asquith became the Liberal Prime Minister. The Liberals' success was attributed to the growing labour movement and a feeling of united fervour against the Conservative government. The Liberals were aware that the mass of the working classes was in distress, and poverty, disease and housing remained concerns. During the election of 1906, they tried to show themselves as the party of concern. The Labour members of Parliament were increasing in number, and were in a position to support or challenge policy. They had the potential backing of the masses and would in time bring the government down. In December 1906,

legislation in the form of the Provision of Meals Act empowered local authorities to provide school meals to needy children. School medical inspections were introduced by the Liberals in 1907. Both these measures were the result of the Physical Deterioration Report of 1904, which showed serious levels of ill health and malnourishment in recruits for the Boer War. From 1912, grants were available for the medical treatment of children. The Children Act of 1908 made it an offence for parents to neglect the health of their children. This Act also changed the way young offenders were dealt with, and included the introduction of *juvenile courts*. Also in 1908, the Old Age Pensions Bill was introduced which advocated a non-contributory system with 5 shillings a week to be paid to the over-70s who were deemed deserving poor. Criminals, drunkards and so-called malingerers could not receive a pension. Pensions were paid through the Post Office, as they are today.

Lloyd George and 'the People's Budget'

Lloyd George was himself from a poor family. He was the first man without wealth or family connection to become Prime Minister of Britain. He was viewed as a leftwing Liberal or 'New Liberal'. He was promoted from the Board of Trade to Chancellor of the Exchequer in 1908. His Budget of 1909 became popularly known as 'the **People's Budget**'. He chose to raise the revenue needed for social reform by increasing the duty on beer, spirits,

tobacco and petrol. He also levied a duty on cars. He introduced a sliding scale for tax, with those on lower incomes allowed to earn a certain amount per child before tax. Those on higher incomes paid a higher rate of tax. He also introduced land duties. These measures obviously hit the middle and upper classes more readily than the working class. Lloyd George called the budget a 'war budget'. It was to raise money for warfare against the 'five giants', poverty, squalor, disease, ignorance and idleness. The budget was part of a dual action, the second being the Town Planning Act. This was introduced by John Burns in 1909. It empowered local authorities to control the development of housing. In both cases, the House of Lords attempted to overthrow them, and in both cases they lost. In 1911, a National Insurance Act was introduced by Churchill, under the guidance of **Sir William Beveridge**, that attempted to deal with the problem of unemployment. (Adapted from Frazer, 1985.)

Influential Idea 5: Fabianism and the rise of the Labour Movement

The Fabian Society was founded in 1834. It took its name from a Roman general Fabius Maximus who was noted for his delaying tactics. The Fabians were a **socialist** group that adopted a gradual approach to reform. They believed that the road to socialism would be a long one, with reform happening over time. The group's members tended to be middle-class intellectuals and academics. Two of its most notable members were Sydney (1859–1947) and Beatrice (1858–1943) Webb. The Webbs wrote many powerful tracts (ie pamphlets) on the social problems of the time. They worked to advance the cause of socialism, and encouraged trade unionisation. They also started the magazine *The New Statesman*.

The **Labour Party** was formed in 1900 as the Labour Representation Committee, its aim to represent trade unions and socialist societies in Parliament. In 1906, 26 of the Party's MPs were elected, and the name was changed to the Labour Party. In 1922, it overtook the Liberals as the main party of opposition. The first Labour government was elected in 1924. It was a minority government, and held office for only 11 months. It was not until 1945 that the Labour Party was elected as a majority government. It was during this period that the welfare state evolved.

'Trade Unions are organised collectives of working people' (Robertson, 1985). They tend to be grouped according to occupation. Until recently, their membership was largely working class. In 1906, **trade union** members were given the legal right to picket and strike. In 1926, the British trade union movement attempted a general strike, but this failed. During the 1980s, former Prime Minister Margaret Thatcher and the then Conservative government eroded the rights enshrined in the 1906 Act and in subsequent legislation. Measures here included: severe restrictions on the right to strike, picket and hold public meetings; the confiscating of funds if members did not comply with the law or if unions openly disobeyed the law; restrictions on the way unions could use the subscriptions they received from their membership; and the end of the 'closed shop' (ie compulsory union membership).

THE PHILANTHROPIC HIGHWAYMAN.

MR. LLOYD-GEORGE. "*I'LL* MAKE 'EM PITY THE AGED POOR!"

Lloyd George's 'People's Budget' was designed to combat the 'five giants' of poverty, squalor, disease, ignorance and idleness

activity

Research the historical background of a trade union of your choice. Make a chart that details its history in chronological (ie date) order. Include pickets, strike actions and any changes in name, status and membership.

The Irish Question

On 13 May 1901, Prime Minister Lord Salisbury ruled out self-government for Ireland. He said that Britain's military power could be undermined by home rule. The Irish Unionists maintained that they would fight any proposal for Irish home rule. The Ulster Protestants wanted to be governed by Westminster, whereas the Ulster Catholics wanted a united Ireland. The political debate raged, and continues to do so, occasionally erupting into violence and civil disorder. Between 1922 and 1972, The Government of Ireland Act (1920) devolved a considerable measure of self-government onto Northern Ireland. The people of Northern Ireland were represented at both Stormont and Westminster. The impact of this was the emergence of separate legislation and social policy in Northern Ireland. In Northern Ireland, for instance, the local authority has less influence and control over the organisation and content of education and the delivery of social services. The province has a completely different set of legal requirements in cases of child protection, with responsibility held centrally through the health boards rather than locally through Social Services as in England and Wales.

The impact of the First World War 1914–18

The First World War was a watershed in social policy. It killed a great many young men, and a whole generation was marked by death and mental and physical disablement. The impact of this war, unlike any other, was felt by all British citizens, for it was not only solders who suffered. At home, coal, rent and food prices were controlled by the state, and by the end of the war, food was rationed. The war served to change the attitudes of a whole generation. Lloyd George realised that the government had to do more to address the conditions of the working class, if social unrest was to be avoided on the soldiers' return from war. A Ministry of Reconstruction was established in 1917. This aimed to bring together the Poor Law provisions, public health authorities, education authorities and insurance commissions. It focused on four main areas:

1 *housing:* one of its first tasks was to provide 'homes fit for heroes'. A programme of construction offered the working class access to improved living conditions. The 'garden city' concept was introduced, with many new houses provided outside the crowded cities. Before 1915, Britain had no recognisable housing policy. Private landlords controlled 90 per cent of the housing stock, with few regulations. In many cases, rents were high and conditions poor. The government had to acknowledge the generally low standard of the housing stock and profiteering by landlords. In 1915, rent controls were introduced, and the concept of a 'fair rent' emerged. The 1919 Housing Act authorised local authorities to build as many houses as possible. By 1939, a million homes had been erected.

2 *health:* at this time, a Ministry of Health was established to draw together the many different policies that influence health care. It attempted to provide more effective health-care provision.

3 *education:* in 1916, H. A. L. Fisher proposed changes to the education system. The Fisher Education Act of 1918 established the principle that all children and young people should have access to education.

4 *poverty:* unemployment was a problem after the war, and an Unemployment Insurance Act was introduced in 1920.

Date	Key development(s)
1832	Great Reform Act
	Business vote
1833	First government grant aid to schools
1834	Poor Law Amendment Act
1838	First Presentation of People's Charter
1842	Chadwick's Report on the Sanitary Conditions of the Labouring Population
1844	District schools for Poor Law children
1846	Pupil–teacher scheme linked to government grants
1847	Poor Law Boards
1848	Final Presentation of People's Charter
	Public Health Act
	General Board of Health established
1851	Common Lodging Houses Act
1852	End of General Health Boards
1854	Reform schools for young offenders
1856	Education Department established
1862	Payment by results in schools
1867	Artisans' vote (skilled workers)
1867	Reorganisation of 'Sick Asylum'
1868	Citizen and Labour Dwellings Act
1870	Foster Education Act (established Local School Boards)
1872	Secret ballot introduced
1872	First Infant Life Protection Act
1875	General Public Health Act
	Artisans Dwelling Act
1876	School Attendance Committees established
1880	Compulsory school attendance
1884	Agricultural workers' vote
1886	Unemployed people employed on public works
1889	Local authority could assume parental rights in cruelty cases
1890	Housing of the Working Classes Act

Date	Key development(s)
1891	Elementary education free to the poor
	Custody of Children Act
1896	Outdoor relief for the aged of good character
1897	Infant Life Protection Act extended to all under-5s
1902	Midwives Act
	Balfour Education Act
1905	Unemployed Workmen Act
1906	School meals for necessitous children
1907	School medical inspections
1908	Pensions for over-70s
1909	Lloyd George's People's Budget
	Beveridge: labour exchanges
	Housing & Town Planning Act
1911	National insurance
1913	Mental Deficiency Act
1914	Rent controls
	Notification of births
1918	Vote for men 21+ and Women 30+
	Maternity and Child Welfare Act
	Fisher Education Act
1919	Addison Housing Act
1920	Unemployment insurance broader scope
1924	Wheatley Housing Act
1928	Votes for women 21+
1930	Greenwood Housing Act
	(slum clearance)
1934	Unemployed Assistance Board

Table 3.1   A historic overview of key social policy

CHAPTER 4

THE WELFARE STATE

The Second World War (1939–45) led to the creation of the **welfare state**. This did not invent or introduce social policy, but drew together a set of policies in a system that had a structure and clearly defined principles. The founding principles of the welfare state were **universalism, statism, egalitarianism, nationalisation** and the redistribution of wealth. It drew together a set of policies designed to combat the 'five giants': ignorance, squalor, poverty, disease and idleness. The main components of the welfare state thus became: education, income maintenance, health, housing and social services.

During the period 1950–70, the phrase 'stop–go' was used to describe the government's development of policy. At times when the economy was buoyant (ie strong), public spending was increased; and at times when it overheated (ie high interest and inflation rates), public spending was controlled.

From 1964, the Labour Party's policies focused on economic prosperity, equality of access to state services, the role of the state in matters of personal relationship, immigration and race relations.

In the early 1970s, it became evident that Britain was heading for recession. The welfare state was costly, and it was impossible to fund the level of service expected by the public from taxation. In 1979, the Conservatives came to power, led by Margaret Thatcher. **Thatcherism** was based on the principles of: decentralisation, privatisation, self-help, competition, freedom of choice, enterprise, individualism and monetarism. Many of the principles enshrined in the 1940s concept of a welfare state were eroded. The policies introduced by Thatcher and consolidated by her successor John Major managed to achieve: a 'safety net' approach to the provision of services; an increase in personal private pension uptake, and in private share ownership; payment by results, increased levels of accountability, a mixed economy of welfare, decentralisation, and increased checks on standards in education and health services.

1997 saw a Labour government for the first time in almost 20 years. The Labour Party became known as 'New Labour' because it accepted the restructuring undertaken by the Conservatives and, with some exceptions, did not intend to change the direction of the welfare state. 'New Labour' under the leadership of Tony Blair, intended to introduce policy reforms that would: provide for more consultation with the public and service providers; promote social inclusion; strengthen the family; promote economic regeneration; give Britain a strong voice in Europe; create Scottish and Welsh Assemblies.

The impact of the Second World War 1939–1945

Richard Titmuss wrote a series of essays discussing the relationship between war and welfare. In his essay 'Problems of social welfare' (1950), he argued that the Second World War created conditions conducive to the development of the welfare state. He believed that the war had brought people together and undermined traditional social groupings related to class, occupation and social status. The war had led to a strong sense of solidarity and a belief that the state had a clear responsibility for the welfare of society. The work of Titmuss has been criticised, and Corelli Barnett, in his work *The Audit of War* (Barnett, 1986), suggests that the decline in Britain's fortunes (as a world power, politically, militarily, economically and technologically) was due to its over-commitment to the welfare state. It is, however, generally agreed that the Second World War heralded a change in both public and political aspirations, the result of which was the welfare state.

It was during the Second World War that a coalition government, led by Winston Churchill, governed Britain. A coalition is where there is no political majority in the House of Commons, but where instead members of different political groups come together. This may occur because no one party can be elected with a majority of votes, or because, as in this case, a common enemy or situation is faced. The effect of the coalition was a shared political vision and an agreement to work together in developing a set of social policies which, when put together, became the welfare state. The postwar election of 1945 saw a Labour government elected, led by Clement Attlee. This upheld the belief that the welfare of society is a collective responsibility of the state.

The growth of the welfare state (1940–48)

The welfare state was established between 1944 and 1948. As we have seen in the previous chapter, the evolution of social policy had been gathering pace, and has a well-documented history. The welfare state did not invent or introduce social policy. What it did do was draw together a set of social policies in a system that had a structure and clearly defined principles.

FOUNDING PRINCIPLES

Universalism

What made the introduction of the welfare state unique in the development of social policy was its commitment to **universalism**. This maintains that all citizens have an equal right to good housing, health care and education. They are also entitled to social security when unable to support themselves financially, and social services when they are unable to support themselves socially and emotionally. Universalism holds that all citizens have a right to free and accessible services.

Statism

The welfare state acknowledged the role of the state in maintaining the health and welfare of its citizens as never before. This **statism** held that the state has an obligation to intervene in any matter that may undermine the welfare of its citizens, including trade and market forces. It is this element of the welfare state that was heavily criticised and 'clawed back' by the policies of the Thatcherite government of the 1990s.

Egalitarianism

Egalitarianism holds that all citizens of a state should be accorded exactly the same rights and privileges. In the welfare state, it generally refers to political rights, ie the right to vote, and to **equality of opportunity**, ie the right to housing, education, health care and an income.

Nationalisation

Nationalisation is the policy of taking firms, enterprises or whole industries into public ownership. The public utilities, such as electricity, gas, water, coal, the fire service, the Post Office and the health services, were all nationalised. Later, telephones, the steel industry and parts of the car industry were similarly nationalised. Nationalisation ensured that all citizens have equal access to such amenities at a reasonable cost. It also shored up jobs, and was a means of controlling public spending.

The redistribution of wealth

The redistribution of wealth occurred by means of the tax system. Those who earned more paid more tax than those on lower incomes. Taxes were used to support the delivery of welfare services. In effect, the richer supported the cost of these services for the poorer.

THE PILLARS OF THE WELFARE STATE: THE 'FIVE GIANTS'

The welfare state drew together a set of policies aimed at combating the 'five giant evils of society', a phrase coined during the 1900s. It was these areas upon which policy was concentrated, and where it established the main components of the welfare state (see Table 4.1).

Giant	Main component of the welfare state
Poverty	Income maintenance (social security)
Ignorance	Education
Disease	National Health Service
Squalor	Housing
Idleness	Social services

Table 4.1 The 'five giant evils of society' and the main components of the welfare state for dealing with them

THE MAIN COMPONENTS OF THE WELFARE STATE

Income maintenance

There are a number of ways in which we can ensure that we have enough money to pay for the things we need. We can work, we can save, buy shares, take out a private pension or life insurance policy or invest in high-cost items like antiques that we hope will increase in value over time. We can use this money to maintain our income in times of shortage. Not everyone has access to this type of saving, however. People may become unemployed, retire or suffer ill health or disablement. The state takes responsibility for maintaining the income of these people through benefits and pensions. The term **social security** is often used to describe the way a society organises its benefit system. This was the term adopted by Britain in the 1940s. Today, we tend to refer to the DSS (Department of Social Security), the department responsible for the benefit system. The social-security system established in the 1940s was the brainchild of Sir William Beveridge (1879–1963). Beveridge was a Liberal, and is hailed as the founding father of the welfare state. Beveridge believed that social policy had a major role to play in ensuring that everyone had employment and thus an income. He had three main areas of interest.

1 Full employment

Beveridge developed the idea of **labour exchanges**. He believed that the lack of information about job availability led to unemployment and poverty. Labour exchanges put people in touch with jobs. In 1924, and again in 1942, he wrote reports that recommended a key role for government if full employment was to be achieved. Labour exchanges were funded by government, and still exist today as *job centres*.

2 Social insurance

As early as 1911, Beveridge was involved in designing legislation that introduced unemployment insurance. In 1942, he wrote a pamphlet called *Insurance For All and Everything*. This contained most of the ideas that later found their way into his report of the same year. He was interested in a system that allowed workers to pay a small contribution from their wages each week in return for insurance cover. They could then claim benefit if they fell ill or became unemployed. This became known as a 'contributory insurance system'. We know this today as *National Insurance contributions*. Beveridge's report to the government in 1942 proposed revolutionary changes and a comprehensive set of measures to tackle poverty. It was instrumental in the formation of a social-security system that made provision for the unemployed, the elderly and the dependent. It included Family Allowance, National Insurance, Sickness Benefit and pensions. Everyone would pay into the scheme and become entitled to receive benefits. Some benefits were provided as of right, not dependent on income, eg Family Allowance (now, Child Benefit) whilst others were means-tested, eg social security (now Income Support).

3 Keynesian theory

In 1936, Beveridge read John Maynard Keynes's *General Theory of Employment, Interest and Money*. This work underpinned many of his ideas. **Keynesianism** held that governments could control the economy. This involved putting money into the economy during a recession, thus increasing the purchasing power of consumers and raising demand. Beveridge used the ideas of Keynes when he developed the social-security system. This style of economics was used by governments to control public spending from the 1940s until the early 1970s when it became unpopular due to recession.

Beveridge's ideas clearly had popular support. George Orwell wrote in 1943 that the great topic of the day was the Beveridge Report: 'People seem to feel that this is a very moderate measure of reform that is almost too good to be true.' The Report was reviewed by most as progressive. However, Beatrice Webb was concerned that the scheme might encourage 'wastrels and spongers'. Beveridge was insistent that the scheme would not discourage thrift and hard work. It was intended to provide 'adequate not generous benefit'. Even in the face of dissent, the Beveridge Report was accepted by the people and government, and was the blueprint for the social-security system then and now.

Education

The reform of the education system was controversial. Before the Second World War, children were either educated in private, largely boarding schools or were reliant on board, church or charity schools. Education generally had to be paid for. Children had to pay a fee, however small, but the greater cost was to the family. If children were in school, they could not work and contribute to the family income. Many church leaders were concerned that state intervention would undermine the importance of religion and the Church. It was **R. A. Butler** (Conservative MP) who finally managed to persuade the Church to agree to the changes. He assured them that religion would not be ignored and would become a compulsory subject in all schools.

The 1944 Education Act provided:

- free and universal provision;
- an end to all age schools;
- a building programme to create primary and secondary schools in every local authority;
- a school-leaving age of 15 years in the first instance, rising to 16 years later on;
- the right for young workers to go to college on day release;
- support for those going to university, in the form of grants and scholarships;
- a compulsory act of Christian religious worship every day unless parents objected.

Health

In 1943, the Ministry of Health drew up a proposal for a National Health Service (the NHS). It said that the service would be free at the point of use and paid for out of national insurance and taxes. The British Medical Association (BMA) objected on the grounds that it would reduce the income of doctors. Doctors liked their independence and did not want to be controlled by local government. In 1944, the White Paper *A National Health Service* was published. **Aneurin Bevan** (1897–1960) (Labour MP) knew the BMA would need to feel safeguarded if the proposal required the nationalisation of services. Bevan managed to push the bill forward, focusing the BMA on the advantages for the profession to get their support.

The 1946 National Health Service Act stated that the service:

- was to be free at the point of delivery and paid for out of taxation;
- would be nationalised;
- required all citizens to register with a doctor of their choice and receive treatment, or be referred to hospital;
- would allow GPs to remain as private professional people but be grouped in partnerships.

Housing

Before the Second World War, most people lived in private rented accommodation, although from 1919 the trend was moving towards local-authority or council housing. Rent controls kept rents at a reasonable level. Many private landlords began to find their business unprofitable, and left it. This worsened the housing shortages as many homes had been lost to the Blitz (bombing). The shortage of building materials after the war meant that four-fifths of building licences in 1948 were granted to local authorities, making council housing the fastest-growing sector at that time.

Personal social services

During the Second World War, children were evacuated from the big cities to avoid the Blitz. They were sent to rural areas that were relatively safe from attack. The evacuation of children highlighted issues of poverty, malnourishment and poor living conditions. Some evacuees and their families were brutally treated by their host families. The death of two boys led to the Monckton Inquiry (1945) which uncovered a number of administrative and professional errors. This led to a greater recognition of abuse. The Curtis Inquiry (1946) considered the plight of children at risk.

The 1948 Children Act led to:

- a separate department for children, created by the local authority;
- a new *social-work* profession, with trained and specialist staff.

At this time, the specific needs of older people, those with mental health problems, the sick and disabled were addressed through social security, health services and charity organisations.

A child is rescued from the rubble of her home during the Blitz of the Second World War

The welfare state: consolidation and containment (1950–76)

It is often argued that the period between 1940 and 1970 was one of political consensus as far as the welfare state was concerned. However, both the Conservative and Labour parties thought quite differently about the appropriate role for the state in issues of welfare. Those in the Labour Party tended towards the view that the state should foster a sense of unity and citizenship; that it should support the family and adhere to traditional moral values. On the other hand, Conservative thinking, whilst accepting the role of the state in ensuring morality, felt that the welfare state would undermine the creativity of individuals and the market. The Conservatives argued strongly for a greater role for home ownership and for the private sector in the provision of housing. Taxes were often used as a means of attacking the social-security system. The Conservative Party favoured *grammar schools*, whilst Labour pushed for *comprehensive* education. The Conservative vision as early as 1951 was to try to contain the welfare state. Once in power (1951–64), they removed rationing and restrictions in the building and manufacturing industries. They also tinkered with some elements of welfare policy. It is for this reason that the school-leaving age of 16 years, enshrined in the 1944 Education Act, did not become a reality until 1971.

STOP–GO POLICIES

It was during this period that the phrase 'stop–go' was coined. This describes a recurrent cycle of events that affects public spending and hence the delivery of welfare services. When the economy was 'overheating' (ie there were high levels of spending) and more goods were being imported than exported, the government had to control public and social spending. In periods when the economy was booming, on the other hand, it could afford to relax and increase public spending. The popularity of the welfare state has put pressure on governments to keep up expenditure regardless of the economic situation. Successive governments would find it difficult to find a balance between the needs of the economy and spending on welfare services. However, no party wanted to be seen to be making cuts in welfare spending as this would affect their election chances.

During 13 years of almost continual Conservative government, controls and food rationing were abandoned, the education system was expanded, social security was more rigorously means-tested and targeted, and more people were looking to own their own homes. Despite the Conservatives' attempt at consolidation and containment, the welfare state continued to cost more. It had proved politically and economically impossible to cut it back or make fundamental changes to it. What became clear is that people wanted lower taxes but no reduction in services (Glennerster, 1995). A Labour government came to power in 1964. Social policy was even more central to the Labour Party's ideology. This party intended to concentrate on the following areas:

Economic prosperity

The Labour Party promised an immediate increase in pensions, and introduced wage-related unemployment and sickness benefits. In order to reduce the stigma of benefits, a system of means-tested supplementary benefits was introduced. Increasingly in the postwar era, women moved into paid employment. It became evident, however, that they were not being paid equally for the same work as their male counterparts. In order to address this and other inequalities, The Sex Discrimination Act of 1975 gave rights to equal access and equal treatment in the workplace. The Equal Pay Acts of 1970 and 1975 anticipated and reinforced this legislation, the latter broadening it out to include men and women. These Acts were further reinforced by the European Equal Pay and Equal Treatment Directives.

Equality of access to state services

The issue of *equality* has always been a difficult one for social policy. In most countries of the world, people are paid differently depending on the job they do. Some have jobs of a higher status than others (eg a doctor), whilst others have low status and are usually low paid (eg a hospital porter). This leads to inequality because the people in higher-paid jobs can afford more than those on lower incomes. In addition, those on higher incomes tend to have more influence over how things should be organised than those in lower-status positions. In a country like Britain, it is accepted that inequalities of wealth exist. The redistribution of wealth via taxation is a legitimate way for the government to effect more equality in the system. Its main aim is to ensure that people were treated equally at the point of delivery.

For instance, the 1980 Black Report highlighted a number of inequalities in the health system. These inequalities were largely related to class. Those said to be 'working class' were generally those with low-status, low-paid, often manual jobs. They were said to be more likely to suffer accident or injury, chronic illness, anxiety or disablement, or to have children who were stillborn or who died in the first year of life. In addition, the system used a middle-class language and style not readily understood by the working class. This group therefore asked fewer questions and was more ready to accept whatever service they were offered. They were less likely to approach the services unless referred by a GP or other professional. In order to address issues such as these, the Labour government, from 1964 onwards, introduced a hospital-building programme and a GP's charter, built more health centres and increased the numbers of health visitors and community nurses. The National Health Service was restructured and made more accountable, with a clearer complaints procedure.

In 1971, as a result of the Seebohm Committee report, a modern social-work profession was created. Rather than have specialist social workers in childcare and probation, social workers would receive a generic training that enabled them to work with a variety of client groups. In 1971, the Central Council for the Education and Training of Social Workers was established. This was to be a general resource for the whole family. It was envisaged that the service would not only work with the abused, sick and disabled but also provide a service to support people in need.

Anthony Crosland (Minister of Education) had a vision of a fairer and more equal society. He wanted to undermine the class divisions that existed in the education system. In the late 1960s a circular, *10/65*, announced the government's intention to abolish selective secondary schools and the *eleven-plus* (an exam taken by children in the last year of primary education to determine entry either to grammar school or secondary school). **Local education authorities** (**LEAs**) had no choice: they had to conform. No permission would be given to build new grammar schools. By 1970, nearly all local authorities were switching to the comprehensive system. In 1971, the school-leaving age was raised to 16 years.

As a result of the Plowden Committee report in 1967, the government encouraged a child-centred, relaxed, informal approach to teaching. In addition, pre-school education was seen as important in areas of disadvantage where the standards achieved by pupils in school were low. In order to enable a greater number of people to benefit from higher education, polytechnics and the Open University were introduced.

The state's role in matters of personal relationships

In the development of social policy, the family was assumed to be a private institution, one in which the state should have no role, save where it was suspected of abusing the children brought up in it. The issue of domestic violence began to be debated in the 1970s. Was there a role for the state in protecting women from violent partners? In 1976, the Domestic Violence and Matrimonial Act allowed people to apply for injunctions which could involve the power of arrest.

activity

1 Organise a class debate. Proposition. 'This house believes that the state has a role in protecting both women and men from violent partners.'
2 Find out about the law in relation to this matter. Who has what rights, and when? What is the role of the police? What kinds of service are available for people who have been victims of domestic violence?

The Wolfenden Report (1957) was the first to question the state's role in the private lives of individuals. It held that there should be no intervention save

> ... to preserve public order and decency, protect the citizen from what is injurious and to provide sufficient safeguards against exploitation and the corruption of others. The law should protect young people, those with some mental defect and any individual from abuse.

The Sexual Offences Act (1967) decriminalised homosexual acts between consenting men over the age of 21 years. However, homosexuality was still deemed publicly unacceptable, and the Act did not undermine existing prejudice or discrimination. Abortion remains a contentious issue too. This was legalised in 1967, but as with homosexuality, the stigma remained. The criteria for abortion were very restrictive, and women often complained of harsh treatment within the NHS. In the period between 1968 and

1991, there were 16 attempts to change the law; none were successful.

The Divorce Reform Act (1969) introduced the 'no fault' divorce. Irretrievable breakdown as a result of adultery, unreasonable behaviour, desertion or separation were the criteria on which a divorce was granted. Then in 1970 the Matrimonial Proceedings Act gave the weaker party rights to property. This was followed by the 1973 Matrimonial Causes Act which addressed financial security in cases of divorce. It also introduced a three-year bar excluding people from seeking a divorce until they had been married for three years.

activity

Research project

1 Find out about the current status of divorce law. How easy do you think it is to get a divorce?
2 What do current statistics tell us about the numbers of people who experience divorce?
3 What are the financial, social and emotional implications of divorce for the following:
   ● men
   ● women
   ● children?
4 Organise a discussion or debate about the experiences of people you know concerning divorce. Do any general impressions or themes emerge?

This raft of legislation makes it clear that the state did indeed see a role for itself in the private lives of individuals but was careful to stay within the bounds outlined in the Wolfenden Report.

Immigration and race relations

The labour shortage in the 1950s led to an increasing trend to recruit people in the West Indies and other Commonwealth countries. As a result, the number of black people residing in Britain increased. Immigration became a political issue, not because of the numbers of people involved but because of the prejudice and discrimination they experienced. The 1965 Race Relations Act defined discrimination as 'treating a person less favourably than another on the grounds of colour, race or ethnic or national origins', and made this 'a civil wrong'. The Act focused on blatant discrimination in public places such as pubs, shops, dance halls and cinemas. It did not deal with housing or employment. These issues were not addressed until the 1976 Race Relations Act. (Adapted from Glennerster, 1995).

MATTERS OF PERSONAL OPINION: CROSS-PARTY ISSUES

Discussion on many of the issues outlined above were not party-political. In many instances, members of various active political parties would come together in debate. Individual parties did not adopt a particular view or introduce a *whip* that required their members to follow the party line. MPs voted as their own conscience dictated in many instances. For this reason, no one party could be said to be responsible for the resulting legislation. However, it is clear that the Labour Party was instrumental in introducing the debate and forwarding the resulting legislation.

Restructuring the welfare state (1976–90)

In the early 1970s, it became evident that Britain was heading towards economic crisis. The welfare state was proving costly, and the economic situation in Britain made it impossible to fund the level of service expected by the public from taxation.

A number of crises undermined the status of the welfare state:

- the oil crisis
- recession
- a sterling crisis (the value of the pound dropped, and Britain was refused a loan from the International Monetary Fund)
- high levels of inflation
- a decline in world trade
- high levels of public spending
- high unemployment
- growing numbers of older people entitled to pensions and services
- public-sector strikes.

The welfare state was criticised as bureaucratic, inefficient, ineffective and wasteful. The Labour government in power during the 1970s decided to cut back on public spending and introduce policy reforms. The Conservatives felt that Labour would not go far enough and based their election campaign on bringing Britain out of recession and the welfare state into line with the resources available. The election in 1979 saw a Conservative victory and the establishment of Margaret Thatcher as Prime Minister. She made it clear that she would cut public expenditure and look critically at the delivery of welfare services.

In Thatcher's government, Keynesian economics was replaced by **monetarist** policies. An American economist Milton Friedman advised the Thatcher government that the way to make Britain wealthy and reduce unemployment was to cut inflation.

The Conservatives developed a new set of policies which were based on the following principles:

- *decentralisation:* this reduces the role of central government or the state in the delivery of welfare services.
- *privatisation:* this enables private companies to own, organise and deliver services once controlled by the state, eg gas, electricity, water, railways, buses and telephones.
- *self-help:* this encourages people to do things for themselves. It also encourages voluntary organisations to become involved in service delivery.
- *competition:* this encourages businesses to offer efficient and cost-effective services if they wish to be successful and not lose custom to competitors. It is believed that competition in business stimulates the economy and provides a greater choice for the consumer.
- *freedom of choice:* this stimulates flexibility and competition in businesses and in organisations such as schools and hospitals. It acknowledges people's right to make decisions about the type of service that best suits their needs.
- *enterprise:* this encourages creativity and

Margaret Thatcher, the former Conservative Prime Minister, after her 1979 General Election victory

innovation. It stimulates a 'culture' that promotes economy, efficiency, effectiveness, responsiveness, rationalisation, competition and choice.

- *individualism:* this suggests that individuals have a responsibility for themselves and for their dependants and should seek to do their individual best by them. It holds that individual needs are of more importance than collective (ie society/community) needs.

The Conservatives quite clearly wanted to halt the growth of the welfare state. Mrs Thatcher, as already mentioned, called it the 'nanny state', insisting that the welfare state created dependency and stifled creativity. In her view, the state should be responsible for providing a 'safety net' via the welfare state for those in genuine need. In order to achieve this aim, the following strategies were introduced:

- monetarism
- flat-rate taxation
- reform of the benefit and social-security system
- housing reform, focusing on home ownership
- education reform, focusing on funding, standards and a **National Curriculum**
- reduced trade-union powers
- privatisation of public utilities and public companies
- a restructuring of the health service
- a crackdown on crime, law and order

- a reduced role for local authorities, and the dissolving of the Greater London Council
- incentives for people to work, eg the Youth Training Scheme (YTS) and the Job Club
- targeting those in genuine need
- strengthening the family and family values
- stiffer penalties for law-breaking.

Between 1979 and 1990, the Thatcher administration was successful in introducing sweeping changes to:

- social policy
- the organisation and delivery of services
- the role of the state in welfare provision.

The political beliefs of this era became known as **Thatcherism**.

The welfare state ... the 1990s and beyond

In order to keep pace with the growing demands of the economy, technology, population trends and public attitudes, the welfare state has evolved and changed. The changes brought about during the 1980s were revolutionary. The Conservatives, led by John Major, continued to build on the success of Thatcherism. The private and voluntary sectors became, and continue to be, increasingly involved in areas that were traditionally the preserve of the welfare state.

The principles that underpinned the emergence of the welfare state in the 1940s had slowly been eroded. The welfare state of the 1990s was characterised by new principles as follows.

- *A 'safety net' approach to service provision.* The state's role in the delivery of welfare services was drastically reduced. The policies of this era reflected a belief that the state's responsibility was to provide services that targeted those in genuine need at a level that did not encourage dependency or undermine self-help. In essence, they provided, again, a 'safety net'.

- *The encouragement of private insurance.* Working people were encouraged to provide for their own pensions, and health-care needs, through private insurance. Companies were given incentives to provide private health insurance for their employees. This period saw the blossoming of private health care, through agencies such as BUPA, and a rise in private pensions.

- *The encouragement of personal wealth creation.* Working people were encouraged to speculate in the marketplace. 'Armchair' share ownership was popularised by the selling off of shares when public utilities and companies were privatised. People queued to buy shares in British Gas, British Telecom and the water authorities. In addition, tax incentives on savings such as TESSA and National Savings Bonds encouraged long-term investment.

- *Payment by results.* The policies of this era witnessed a move towards *productivity bonuses* as a means of rewarding hard work. Payment by outcomes began to characterise the funding of both education and the health service.

- *Accountability.* Service providers were made more openly accountable. Schools and National Health Trusts had to publish their results. The 'league table' has become commonplace alongside the **charter** and the **mission statement**. Service providers are expected to provide clear guidelines for service users. Most large organisations have a mission statement which tells people what the broad aim of the organisation is. Some have a charter which tells the service user exactly what they can expect.

activity

1 Find out if your college/employer has a mission statement. Do you agree with what it says?
2 Request a copy of the relevant charters from your local
   - National Health Service Trust
   - railway
   - water authority.
   What are the similarities and differences in these?
3 In small groups, write a mission statement and charter for your faculty, department or organisation.

- *A 'mixed economy' of welfare.* The policies of this era reflected the idea of a 'mixed economy' of welfare, ie a welfare system that emphasises the diversity of provision and the potential for a number of different providers to be involved in the delivery of that service, the state's role again being to offer a 'safety net' service for those who could not afford to pay for such a service themselves. This concept also acknowledges the role of the voluntary sector and charities in providing services in place of the state for those in need.
- *Raising standards.* The policies of this era reflected the government's belief that standards in education were undermining the ability of Britain to compete favourably with other developed nations. The National Curriculum, Standard Attainment Tests (SATs), changes to both the GCSE and A-level syllabi and to National Vocational Qualifications were all aimed at raising the educational standards of the future workforce.
- *Decentralisation.* The policies of this era gave people greater choice. Parents were theoretically able to choose their children's school, and Nursery Vouchers enabled parents to choose and pay for their children's pre-school education. Schools were able to opt out of local-authority control and access their funding directly, giving them more flexibility in the way they spent their grant. Similar policies affected the health service, with the emergence of trusts, more choice being given to patients, and changes to the funding of GP practices. The effect of these measures was to erode the role of the local education and health authorities.

The Conservative government remained in power for almost two decades. The election in 1997 was overshadowed by a split in the party around Britain's membership of the European Union and the idea that all members use a single currency. The Conservatives were defeated in the 1997 election by an overwhelming Labour majority.

'NEW LABOUR' (BLAIRISM)

Just as the welfare state has evolved over time, so have political parties. It has been argued that the shift in Labour's ideology has been the more profound. Traditionally, the Labour Party's beliefs were based on a socialist ideology, an ideology that emphasised:

- egalitarianism (equality)
- a central role for the state in providing welfare services (**institutional welfare**)
- **collectivism** (working for the good of society/community, not the individual)
- **unionism** (the collective voice of the workforce).

The Thatcherite policies that spanned almost two decades changed the public's attitudes, values and expectations. The trade unions experienced a declining membership, the role of local government had been cut back, people became wealthier and a culture of 'individualism' had replaced the importance of community. It was impossible for the Labour Party to remain wedded to traditional socialism. Under the leadership of Tony Blair, 'New Labour' emerged. This accepted the need for a restructuring of the welfare state. Tony Blair did not want to alienate the public, and reassured it that many of the policies put in place during the Conservative government would stay in place. The reforms proposed sought to:

- provide for wider public consultation before policy decisions were made
- promote 'social inclusion'
- strengthen the family and family values
- encourage wealth creation
- establish assemblies in Scotland and Wales
- establish Britain as a powerful voice in the European Union.

Scotland and Northern Ireland

For historic reasons, both Scotland and Northern Ireland have enjoyed some self-government. For this reason, legislation and social policy in these countries have not directly mirrored that in England and Wales. In most cases, the broad themes and concepts are the same, but the implementation and organisation of those themes differ.

In 1972, the Northern Ireland (Temporary Provisions) Act suspended Stormont and imposed direct rule from Westminster. In 1974, an attempt was made to restore self-government through a new Northern Ireland Executive elected by proportional representation, the aim being to give both Protestants and Catholics a voice in the decision-making process. This did not work, and the government of Northern Ireland is now channelled through a Secretary of State for Northern Ireland at Westminster who heads a Northern Ireland Office. The departments responsible for social care and service delivery are the responsibility of the Northern Ireland Office.

Scotland's affairs are also channelled through a Secretary of State for Scotland

Date	Government	Social Security	Health	Education	Housing	Social Services
1940	Coalition	Assistance Board				
1941	Coalition	Abolition of household means-test				
1942	Coalition	Beveridge Report: social insurance				
1944	Coalition			Butler Education Act		
1945	Labour	Family allowances. Wages Council Act				
1946	Labour	National Insurance Act	National Health Service Act	Education Act	New Towns Act. Furnished House (Rent Control) Act	
1947	Labour				Town and country planning	
1948	Labour	National Assistance Act				Children Act
1949	Labour				Local authority housing not restricted to the working class	Legal Aid and Advice Act
1950	Labour					Matrimonial Causes Act
1951	Labour		Charges for dentures and glasses			Services set up for deaf and physically disabled

Date	Government	Social Security	Health	Education	Housing	Social Services
1952	Conservative	Increases in national insurance and assistance	Prescription charges		Sale of council houses with ministerial permission	Children Act (taking children into care)
1953	Conservative		Labour proposes comprehensive schools			
1954	Conservative	National insurance increase		Report on Early Leaving	Housing Repairs and Rents Act	
1956	Conservative		Guillibaud Report on the cost of the NHS		Slum clearance	Piercy Report on the Rehabilitation, Training and Resettlement of Disabled Persons. Sexual Offences Act
1957	Conservative	National insurance increase. Introduction of Superannuating			Rent Act	
1958	Conservative	Provision for Old Age (White Paper)				Disabled Persons (Employment) Act. Children Act (fostering and adoption). Matrimonial Causes (Property and Maintenance) Act. Matrimonial Proceedings (Children) Act

Date	Government	Social Security	Health	Education	Housing	Social Services
1959	Conservative	National Insurance Act	Mental Health Act	Crowther Report		Young Husband Report (social work)
1960	Conservative					Matrimonial Proceedings (Magistrates Courts) Act
1961	Conservative				Parker Morris Report (Homes for Today and Tomorrow)	
1962	Conservative		Porrit Report (Medical Services Review) Hospital Plan			Health Visitors and Social Work Training Act
1963	Conservative			Newsom Report (Half Our Future)		Children and Young Persons Act. Community development initiatives. Matrimonial Causes Act
1964	Conservative	Family Allowance and National Insurance Act			Housing Act (improvement areas)	Married Women's Property Act
1965	Labour			Plans for changing comprehensive system	Milner Holland Report. Rent Act. The Housing Programme (White Paper)	The Child, the Family and the Young Offender (White Paper). Matrimonial Causes Act. Abolition of death penalty

Date	Government	Social Security	Health	Education	Housing	Social Services
1966	Labour	National Insurance Act Ministry of Social Security Act			Rating Act (rent rebates)	
1967	Labour			Plowden Report (primary education)	Housing Subsidies Act (mortgage option scheme)	Sexual Offences Act. Matrimonial Homes Act. Abortion Act
1968	Labour		Structure of NHS (Green Paper)		Rent Act	Seebohm Report (structure of social services). Children in Trouble (White Paper)
1969	Labour	National Superannuation and Social Insurance (White Paper)			Renovation of Older Houses and Housing Act.	Children and Young Persons Act. Family Law Reform Act. Divorce Reform Act
1970	Labour	National Insurance (Old Person's and Widows Pensions and Attendance Allowance) Act. Family Income Supplement Act. Equal Pay Act	Structure of NHS (Green Paper)			Local Authority Social Services Act. Matrimonial Proceedings and Property Act
1971	Conservative	Industrial Relations Act				
1973	Conservative	Social Security Act. Employment Act				Matrimonial Causes Act

Date	Government	Social Security	Health	Education	Housing	Social Services
1974	Conservative/ Labour		Reorganisation of health service		Housing Act	Rehabilitation of Offenders Act
1975	Labour	Social Security Benefits Act. Social Security Pensions Act. Child Benefit Act. Employment Protection Act. Equal Pay Act				Sex Discrimination Act
1976	Labour			Education Act		Race Relations Act. Domestic Violence and Matrimonial Proceedings Act. Sexual Offences (amendment) Act
1978	Labour	Employment Act				Matrimonial and Family Proceedings Act
1980	Conservative	Employment Act			Housing Act	
1981	Conservative			Education Act		
1982	Conservative	Employment Act	Reorganisation of the health service			
1984	Conservative					Matrimonial and Family Proceedings Act
1986	Conservative	Social Security Act				Sex Discrimination Act

Date	Government	Social Security	Health	Education	Housing	Social Services
1988	Conservative	Local Government Act. Local Government Finance Act	Working for Patients (White Paper)	Education Reform Act	Housing Act	
1989	Conservative				Local Government and Housing Act	Children Act
1990	Conservative	Employment Act	National Health Service and Community Care Act. Human Fertilisation and Embryology Act	Education (Students Loans) Act		
1991	Conservative	Child Support Act				
1993	Conservative	Trade Union Reform and Employment Rights Act		Education Act (code of practice for children with special educational needs)		
1997	Conservative			Nursery voucher scheme		
1997	Labour			Education Bill (education reform)		
1998	Labour	New Deal. Welfare to Work Programme		National Childcare Strategy		Sure Start. Quality Protect (White Paper: Review of Social Services)

Table 4.2   The welfare state: key policy chart

and a separate Scottish Office which is split into several departments. Social care and service delivery are controlled by local government. Social services, housing and education are regulated by separate legislation. The health service maintains a strong link to the English system but differs in its structure.

HOUSING

In Ireland, social housing is common. This is organised by a province-wide Housing Executive (provinces being like counties). Similarly, most housing in Scotland is provided by public housing authorities and local authorities.

HEALTH

In Scotland, health boards at both regional and local levels organise the delivery of services. In Northern Ireland, there are four health and social-services boards with area responsibilities. The management of health services broadly reflects the English and Welsh system.

EDUCATION

In Scotland, Wales and Northern Ireland, all education (except for higher education) is the responsibility of the Scottish, Welsh and Northern Ireland Offices. In Northern Ireland, most pupils attend denominational schools based on their religion.

CHAPTER 5

SOCIAL CARE AND SERVICE DELIVERY

The state has three main roles in the delivery of services: as a regulator, as a funder and as a planner/provider.

Anything that has to do with policy is based on value judgements. One of the most significant values to underpin British social policy is a belief in helping those who are unable to care for or help themselves. Titmuss referred to this in two ways: **altruism**, which is linked to moral obligation and duty; and the *gift relationship*, based on the concept of *reciprocity*. Certain values underpin the direct delivery of services to the public; these include: a caring ethos, empowerment and respect for personal privacy and dignity.

Services are delivered by the **public, private, voluntary** and **informal** sectors.

The Community Care Act 1990 underpins policies that promote care in the community both in formal (day-centre) and in informal (home) settings. Now additional legislation insists that the needs of the carer as well as the cared-for person be taken into account in any assessment process.

Britain is said to have a **mixed economy of welfare**, ie one in which the state does not provide all the services but works in conjunction with the other sectors. **Welfare pluralism** is the provision of services by a number of different providers working independently or in partnership.

There are three main distinctions in service delivery: *functional division, client groups* and *area-based divisions*.

Organisations are increasingly adopting a corporate approach to service delivery.

There are three main approaches to service delivery: *reactive, systematic* and *comprehensive*.

Partnership working is of vital importance in the delivery of social welfare services. Where the various sectors and organisations can effect positive working relationships and can agree on their approaches to the relevant issues, problems and service requirements, a more comprehensive and effective service for the user is made possible. An organisation has a *culture* based on its past and present structure, function and philosophy. Partnership working can be made difficult if organisations have very different cultures.

The delivery of social welfare involves a number of different occupational groups with very different cultures, roles and responsibilities.

The role of the state in the delivery of social care

According to Michael Hill (1996), the state has three main roles.

1 *Regulator.* As a regulator, the state does not leave decisions about education, health care, housing or income maintenance to individuals. Legislation is one way in which the state sets the ground rules for service delivery. Another is through circulars. These give guidance to service providers, such as county councils, about how services should be organised.

   Inspection is another form of regulation. OFSTED is the mechanism through which schools are regulated, OFWAT the mechanism through which electricity companies are regulated, and OFTEL regulates the telecommunications industry. Social Services has traditionally been responsible for the registration and inspection of preschool provision for children, and for homes for the disabled, older people and children in its care.

2 *Funder.* The state, through a variety of mechanisms, funds service delivery. For instance, it funds state education, health care as delivered by the NHS Trusts, GP services, some dental and eye treatment, the benefit system, personal social services, the fire service, the police and some areas of the criminal justice system. These services are funded through:
   - taxation
   - national insurance
   - the National Lottery
   - investment
   - income from selling services, eg private beds in NHS hospitals.

Funds are drawn down by these services in various and often complicated manners. Schools, for instance, can be funded in a number of ways:
   - by the local education authority from monies given by central government;
   - by grants obtained directly from central government (ie as with grant-maintained schools);
   - by grants obtained directly from the local education authority (ie through Local Management of Schools: LMS)

3 *Planner and provider.* The state is responsible for making sure that adequate education, health services, benefits and housing are available. It takes a lead role in developing policies that affect the way in which these services are organised and provided. It is responsible for ensuring that future as well as present needs are addressed. It has to plan what is needed, and when, where and what policies or changes to policy are needed to make this happen. This may involve encouraging private and voluntary organisations to become involved in service delivery.

   Example: it is estimated that Britain requires a further 4 million homes to be built in the next decade if housing shortages are to be avoided. The government has set targets for all county councils.

activity

Visit the Planning Office that is responsible for the area in which you live. On display or by request, you are entitled to see the plans for your local area. Do these indicate expansion? If so, by how much, and where? How many new homes are expected to be built in the next 10 years? Who is expected to build these homes?

Values and choices in social care

Richard Titmuss contested that there was no escape from value choices in 'welfare systems'. Anything that has to do with policy must, he said, be inevitably concerned with 'what is and what might be; with what we (as members of a society) want (the ends); and how we get there (the means)' Policy decisions are by their very nature *value judgements*.

A value is the worth or desirability of a thing. Value can indicate the worth of something in money, but in this case we are talking of worth in terms of its importance or significance to us socially and psychologically. A value judgement is a personal estimate of worth. A political belief, in its own way, is a value judgement: you believe in the ideas upheld by a particular party. When you vote, we are saying you agree with the values enshrined in the policies of your chosen party. The beliefs of individuals, society and other nations all influence the development of policy and service delivery. The New Deal, for instance, is an American idea and has informed strategies to promote employment and get people off benefits. The values underpinning this system are essentially American.

One of the most significant values to underpin social care in Britain is a belief in helping those who are unable to care for themselves, namely the sick, older people, children and disabled people. Titmuss characterised this in two ways:

1 *Altruism.* This is the principle of unselfish regard for the needs and interests of others. **Altruism** is based on notions of moral obligation and responsibility. We freely accept that some of our taxes will support those unable to support themselves for reasons beyond their control. We freely give to charities or undertake voluntary work for the same reasons.

2 *The gift relationship.* This is the principle of unselfishly giving to others, based on the concept of *reciprocity*. Titmuss used the example of blood donations to explain this principle. People, he said, give blood not from some altruistic notion of moral obligation but because we never know when we ourselves may be in need of this service. We give now in order to receive later, and this he called reciprocity.

The argument that values influence policy is equally true of service delivery:

● *The caring ethos.* When we go into hospital, we want or need to believe that the people delivering the service care about what they are doing. We form relationships with those delivering the service, eg doctors, nurses, midwives and health visitors. We expect these people to be professional and know what they are doing, but more than that, we expect their respect and kindness. We expect them to care about us. This can pose difficulties. If a patient is terminally ill and dying of cancer, should the doctor turn a blind eye if that person's choice is to take their own life? And if they involve others in that choice? What if the patient asks for the doctor's help in carrying out their own wishes? Is it more or less caring to respect the wish of this person? Inevitably, the doctor concerned has to make a value judgement, knowing that the law could find them guilty of murder.

- *Privacy and dignity.* The delivery of services is bound by charter to respect the dignity of service users by acknowledging their wishes, listening to what they say, giving them adequate information and respecting their lifestyle choices and cultural and religious beliefs. Privacy is respected in two ways, one in a physical sense, making sure, for instance, that those in hospital or residential accommodation have access to a lockable bathroom. The other is in respect of the information held about them. People have a right to confidentiality and for information about them to be shared only with those who need to know. Best practice would require that they know who these people are. Information should be kept in a safe place, with no public access. In addition, the law allows people to challenge information held about themselves.

- *Empowerment.* To be empowered, we need:
  - access to information
  - choice
  - a role in any decision-making process that affects us
  - respect.

---

activity

Consider the following. What are the issues of confidentiality involved, and how should they be handled? Who do you think should have access to the information here?

- Jill is four years old. She has told the nursery nurse at her pre-school that her father sexually abuses her. Social Services has been informed, and it is undertaking an investigation jointly with the police.
- Mrs Khan is 80 years old and lives in residential accommodation. She was recently told she has an untreatable cancer and less than a year to live. She has asked her key worker and daughter to contact EXIT, an organisation that believes in the right of individuals in such circumstances to end their lives.
- Mr Coombs has been diagnosed HIV positive. He is a dentist.
- Mrs Smy is coming round from a general anaesthetic. She begins to ramble and talks of her job as a finance clerk. She tells the nurse that she has embezzled £30,000 during the last five years of her employment.

Empowerment enables us to take control of our own lives and of issues that directly affect them. Policies have a role in empowering the socially excluded or disadvantaged. Women have been empowered by the Sex Discrimination and Equal Pay Acts, European Directives and National Childcare Strategy. Those with mental health problems are protected by the 1983 Mental Health Act, and children by the Children Act 1989. Legislation and policy can only empower people so far, however. It can only address discrimination in broad terms, and much that denies people power is not openly displayed. It can be in the mannerisms of individuals, the way that a waiting room is organised, the language used by practitioners, the kinds of magazines left out whilst you wait your turn.

Advocacy is a growing movement. This is a means by which those who find it difficult to put their own case or express their own needs can do so through another. This person acts on their behalf or accompanies them to lend support.

activity

In threes, role-play the role of advocate:

- Person 1 is a social worker;
- Person 2 is a young man with a learning difficulty and speech impairment;
- Person 3 is the advocate.

Person 2 is unhappy with the group home he has recently joined. He knows that the social worker put a lot of effort into getting him a place, so he feels guilty about complaining. Nevertheless, he is unhappy and yet unsure how to explain how he feels.

After the role play, discuss the way each person approached the situation. List the things that each person had to consider. Did Person 2 feel powerless during the role play? How did the advocate and social worker ensure that Person 2 did not feel powerless in this situation? In the light of this discussion, replay the role play, and afterwards discuss what you did differently and why.

The delivery of social care services

THE PUBLIC SECTOR

The **public sector** is that part of service delivery that is funded and managed by the state. The state:

- maintains minimum universal standards (as regulator)

- maintains the status quo through social control and social engineering (as planner)
- ensures adequate service provision (as planner/funder/provider).

The services provided in this sector are often referred to as *statutory services*, ie they are provided as of statute, that is by law. For instance, the law states that all children are entitled to free formal education from the school term in which they are five years of age. The Education Department must ensure that enough places are available here. Those agencies that provide these services are often referred to as **statutory agencies**. Only one voluntary organisation in Britain has statutory responsibility. This is the National Society for the Prevention of Cruelty to Children (NSPCC). No private company has statutory responsibility. Not having statutory responsibility does not mean that the private and voluntary sectors can ignore the law. What it means is that these sectors can choose what services they want to offer and at what level, unlike Social Services, the health service, the Education Department and the DSS.

THE PRIVATE SECTOR

There is a growing trend towards the delivery of services by private businesses, companies and corporations – ie the **private sector**. These provide services for profit. BUPA, for instance, provides health-care services including hospital treatment. Individuals have to pay for these services. Usually, they take out an insurance or are covered by a company policy. Sometimes, the state pays on the individual's behalf. For instance, Social Services might pay a private residential home to care for an older or disabled person. Generally speaking, they pay for services only when it is cheaper than providing them themselves, or when a service is not available in an area.

THE VOLUNTARY SECTOR

The voluntary sector is very diverse. Some voluntary organisations are small and locally based, whilst others are large, professional agencies. They undertake a range of activities:

● direct service delivery
● self-help and support groups
● **pressure groups** and advocacy.

They tend to target particular needs or groups of people. The RNIB (Royal National Institute for the Blind) provides services for the blind and partially sighted. Age Concern targets the retired. The Cystic Fibrosis Foundation concentrates on one specific genetic disease.

Voluntary organisations are becoming increasingly involved in the delivery of social care services. They are funded to do this in a variety of ways, ie via:

● public and corporate donations
● trusts, covenants and inheritance
● the National Lottery
● grants from central or local government
● service line agreements with local government departments.

Paul Spiker (1995) maintains that the organisation of these services differs depending on the type of activity or group they provide for. Those working in health and disablement tend to be hierarchical and conservative in their approach. Those working in housing and community work tend to be participative and progressive in their approach.

activity

Reproduce and complete the chart below for organisations active in your local area:

Voluntary organisation	Type of activity	Target group/issue	Local/national

THE INFORMAL SECTOR

The **informal sector** consists of friends, family, neighbours and communities. A great deal of social care is discharged not by professionals but by informal networks. This type of care has always happened: parents caring for children, children caring for parents, families caring for sick and disabled members; local communities caring for each other: shopping for a neighbour, babysitting, feeding the cat whilst people are away etc. The National Child Care Strategy recognises for the first time the role of the family in providing informal care. Policies linked to this strategy are designed to facilitate this type of care for the first time in the childcare field. It also acknowledges the reality that most informal care is shored up by women. The state has also reinforced the role of the informal sector through the implementation of **community care**.

COMMUNITY CARE

The Community Care Act 1990 underpins policies that promote care in the community. Community care relates not just to care by informal networks but also to the provision of services for the mentally ill, the disabled and older people in local communities. Rather than providing for the care of these groups in institutions on the fringes of towns and cities, this Act promoted their closure and encouraged small-scale units to be set up on housing estates, in villages and in town centres. The Act was an attempt to address a growing concern about the negative effects of 'institutionalisation'. It held that those living away from their families and outside of the local community were isolated and stigmatised. The regime within institutions such as mental hospitals was based largely on the needs of staff (shift patterns, working conditions), and these hospitals were often too large to feel homely. Community care was seen as more respecting of the individual, enabling them to have a 'normal lifestyle'. The government argued that this would be more cost-effective and less psychologically damaging to individuals. The concept itself of community care is not flawed, but its implementation has been heavily criticised for being under-resourced, with a lack of staff to monitor and support those living in the community. The killing of Jonathan Zito, in North London, by schizophrenic Christopher Clunis in 1993 led to an inquiry and debate about what was appropriate care in the community. It called for the provision of more hospital beds for psychiatric patients, particularly in certain parts of London.

The carers

A survey of carers found that more than a quarter had not heard of community care, with three-quarters maintaining that no assessment had been made on the person for whom they cared. Carers expressed concerns about the level of support for themselves as well as for those for whom they care (according to the National Association of Carers). Legislation is now in place that gives carers some right to respite from services and support. Assessments should reflect their own needs as well as those of the person being assessed. Feminists have criticised community care for putting an additional burden on women in the community. They argue that most people working in the caring occupations are women, and that in addition they form the majority of carers in the informal care sector. When the government asks the community to care, is it really asking women to care?

activity

Organise a debate. Proposition: 'Men care when they have to, women care because they are expected to.'

WELFARE PLURALISM

It is clear that the state does not provide all social care services but works in conjunction with other providers in a mixed economy of welfare. **Welfare pluralism** is the provision of services from many different sources. It is argued that welfare pluralism promotes diversity, with a greater range of services offered which cater for individual needs and choice. Welfare pluralism recognises the limitation of the state in providing welfare services. It is argued, however, that welfare pluralism does not provide a comprehensive service. It is inevitable that some needs will not be met. In addition, it may work in favour of some people more than others. Whatever the arguments, however, for the foreseeable future welfare pluralism is here to stay.

THE ORGANISATION OF SERVICE DELIVERY

The administration of services can be complex. There are three main distinctions between different types of service organisation:

1 *functional divisions.* Here, distinctions are made on the basis of what a service does. The main service areas in social care are categorised as health, housing, social security, social work and education. This division in service terms works reasonably well and has a long

tradition in the European Union. However, service boundaries do overlap, and so more and more policies emphasise the need for the different service areas to work in partnership.

2 *client groups.* Here, distinctions are made on the basis of the client group involved. Services might only respond to particular groups of people: older people, children, disabled people etc. Social workers, for instance, do a similar job for all these groups, yet they might work with only one of these groups, ie they might specialise. General practitioners, on the other hand, are generic. They work with all people, their focus being their health and well-being. Their client group are those who suffer ill health.

3 *area-based divisions.* Here, distinctions are made on the basis of geography. Geographic divisions are responsible for the co-ordination of services in their area. The area covered shapes the response of the service. The requirements of a service in an urban area where the population density is high will be quite different from the requirements in a rural area where the population density is low and widely dispersed.

(This section has been adapted from Paul Spiker, 1995.)

activity

List the kinds of services that would be required by a child whose cerebral palsy results in immobility.

Then, divide a large sheet of paper in half. On one side, write 'Lives in urban area', on the other 'Lives in a rural area'.

Look at your list of services. On your sheet of paper, list those that could be offered for children in an urban area and those in a rural area. What are the issues for the delivery of services for children in either area?

A CORPORATE APPROACH

Historically, corporations have been large business organisations. They are usually made up of a number of individual companies, overseen and managed by a parent company or corporation. Corporations might be multi-national, that is they have offices and companies all over the world. Corporations are said to have a particular ethos and way of doing things, and they expect all of the workforce to comply. It acts, if you like, as one individual. Mitsubishi, when setting up business in the north of England, expected its employees to behave as their Japanese counterparts did, including starting the day with exercises. The growth in '**corporatism**' has led to the emergence of corporate thinking in public services. This trend has been encouraged by social policy. In the late 1990s, further-education colleges became corporations. This required them to operate as businesses rather than as a public service. The government changed the way they were funded, and profit became for the first time an issue. A college now has to be competitive to survive; if not, it will close. The health service, Social Services and

Education are expected to organise their services along corporate lines and encourage corporate thinking in their employees. For instance, individual departments have to pay each other for services. Individual departments are required to see themselves as individual companies of one parent organisation, with Social Services and Education sharing the same parent, namely a county council, unitary authority or metropolitan borough.

DECENTRALISATION

Decentralisation is the term used to describe the delegation of service responsibility from national/local government to smaller areas (divisions) or organisations, eg schools and GP surgeries. Elcock (1993, cited by Spiker, 1995) distinguishes three types:

1 *departmental decentralisation:* here, departments devolve their responsibilities to area offices. Social Services often uses this model.
2 *corporate decentralisation:* here, several departments work together to produce comprehensive service delivery in a given area. The health service often adopts this model, with health services in primary health care, eg GPs, health visitors, community nurses, dentists and pharmacists, housed together in *health centres.*
3 *political decentralisation:* here, the emphasis is on 'local', with the idea of empowering communities. Housing Action Trusts often use this model to encourage participation and political representation.

APPROACHES TO DELIVERY

- *A reactive approach:* this involves dealing with problems or situations as they arise. Child-protection issues sometimes fit this category.
- *A systematic approach:* this involves looking at the total needs of an individual within a particular area of service. The housing department can deal with the allocation of housing, emergency housing, rents, rent control in the private sector, and housing benefit. A person can go to the housing office/department and find out what they need to know or do.
- *A comprehensive approach:* here, a framework of services is provided to meet a range of needs. Examples of this approach can be found in health, education, social services and social-security systems.

PARTNERSHIP AND 'JOINED-UP THINKING'

Much newly conceived social policy and supporting legislation since 1989 has included a partnership ethos. The first time working in partnership was defined in law was through the Children Act 1989. This quite clearly states that the protection of children is no one department's responsibility but the responsibility of all the agencies that come into contact with the child. The guidance document *Working Together* sets criteria for the police, health services, education and social services. It brings them together in Area Child Protection Committees (ACPCs) in order to ensure 'joined-up thinking' (ie everyone sharing their views and agreeing on decisions). It is responsible for the joint training of those working with children, and for monitoring the implementation of services by the agencies involved. The belief in the value of partnerships and of joined-up thinking is becoming increasingly evident. Such partnerships have been extended to include the general public and service users by way of charters, strengthened complaints procedures and consultation. The National Childcare Strategy (1998) requires the development of 'Childcare Partnerships' in all the counties of England and Wales. These partnerships are to include representatives from any agency that has contact with children, eg the Pre-school Learning Alliance, the National Childminders Association, schools, the Church and private service providers. It also requires parental representation.

The role of personnel in social care

THE ORGANISATIONAL ENVIRONMENT

Most statutory, private and voluntary organisations are hierarchical in structure. That is, they involve a chain of command and responsibility, with those people at the top having more status and power than those at the bottom (see Figure 5.1). Some smaller organisations, chiefly in the voluntary sector, are organised as *co-operatives*. All members of a co-operative have a voice in the decision-making process, and no one person's role is deemed more important, or has more status, than another's.

Bureaucracy

The sociologist Max Weber characterised **bureaucracy** as a set of basic organisational principles:

- a clear hierarchy representing a chain of command
- salaried staff whose rewards come from their salaries not their positions
- individuals' authority within the organisation coming from their roles
- appointments to posts determined by professional skill and competence
- strict rules about decision-making
- maintained records.

Most large companies and statutory agencies could be described as bureaucracies.

Collectives

A **collective** is any group of co-operating individuals who might produce goods or services together. There is no hierarchy: people retain their own shares and are tied by no bond other than a shared interest in the work of the collective. Members of the collective take on a 'collective responsibility' for the success of the organisation. Decisions are made by vote at members' meetings. People can choose their own role or job within the organisation. This kind of organisational structure is largely confined to small businesses, such as collective farms, wholefood shops and catering services. In the delivery of social care, examples can be found in the housing sector, such as group homes or Housing Action Trusts, and in the form of *credit unions* (where people put money in and can take out loans).

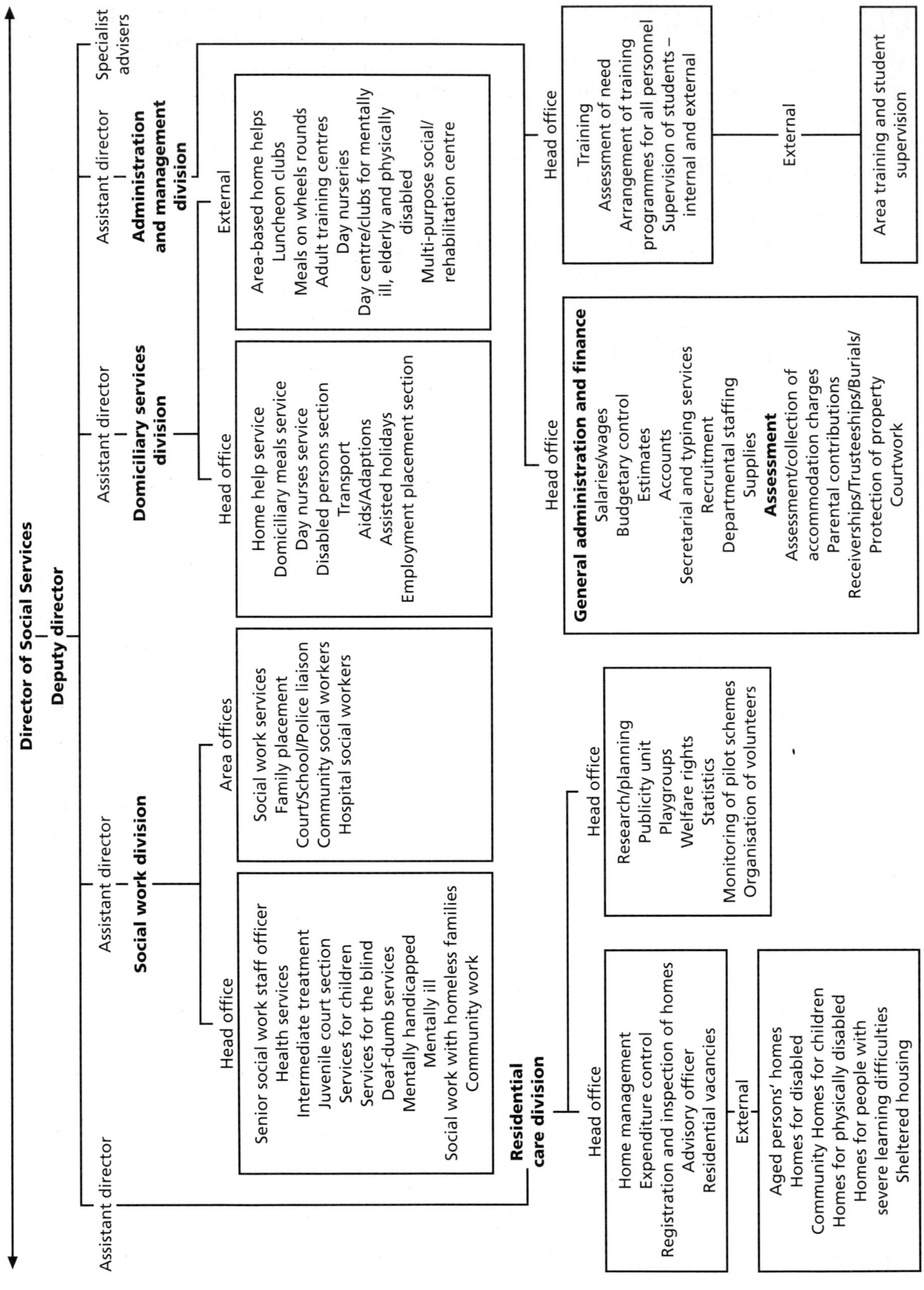

Director of Social Services

Deputy director

Assistant director

Assistant director

Social work division

Head office

Senior social work staff officer
Health services
Intermediate treatment
Juvenile court section
Services for children
Services for the blind
Deaf-dumb services
Mentally handicapped
Mentally ill
Social work with homeless families
Community work

Area offices

Social work services
Family placement
Court/School/Police liaison
Community social workers
Hospital social workers

Residential care division

Head office

Home management
Expenditure control
Registration and inspection of homes
Advisory officer
Residential vacancies

External

Aged persons' homes
Homes for disabled
Community Homes for children
Homes for physically disabled
Homes for people with severe learning difficulties
Sheltered housing

Head office

Research/planning
Publicity unit
Playgroups
Welfare rights
Statistics
Monitoring of pilot schemes
Organisation of volunteers

Assistant director

Domiciliary services division

Head office

Home help service
Domiciliary meals service
Day nurses service
Disabled persons section
Transport
Aids/Adaptions
Assisted holidays
Employment placement section

General administration and finance

Head office

Salaries/wages
Budgetary control
Estimates
Accounts
Secretarial and typing services
Recruitment
Departmental staffing
Supplies
Assessment
Assessment/collection of accommodation charges
Parental contributions
Receiverships/Trusteeships/Burials/
Protection of property
Courtwork

Assistant director

Administration and management division

External

Area-based home helps
Luncheon clubs
Meals on wheels rounds
Adult training centres
Day nurseries
Day centre/clubs for mentally ill, elderly and physically disabled
Multi-purpose social/rehabilitation centre

Specialist advisers

Head office

Training
Assessment of need
Arrangement of training programmes for all personnel
Supervision of students – internal and external

External

Area training and student supervision

Figure 5.1

Organisational culture

All organisations have their own *culture*. This is a set of beliefs, behaviours, rituals and attitudes associated with a particular group of people or organisation. The culture of an organisation will be influenced by:

- legislation and policy
- the nature of the service sector (ie whether statutory, private or voluntary)
- the size of the organisation
- the structure of the organisation
- the service being delivered
- the environment (geographical, physical and financial)
- the goals and objectives of the organisation
- the professional/occupational background of the employees
- the personal and professional influences of the employees
- the style of management adopted by the organisation
- the style of communication adopted by the organisation
- public and professional accountability
- the gender of the workforce
- the client group
- prevailing public expectations
- corporate beliefs and attitudes
- individual employees' beliefs and attitudes
- technology
- the organisation's relationship to other organisations, including government.

The culture of an organisation is important in understanding the decisions it makes about service delivery and service users. If the culture of one organisation, say the health service, is significantly different from that of another, say Social Services, this might pose problems when they work in partnership. It might present invisible barriers for the service user and for professionals working together. It is partly for this reason that social policy has begun to address the issue of partnership in a much more explicit way, and to encourage corporatism.

Occupational groups in social care

Administrators

Administrators exist at all levels of an organisation. Those at the highest level in an organisation develop policy, direct the implementation of service delivery, make decisions about resource allocation, monitor quality control, and sit on boards and committees. They are usually highly qualified professionals with a lot of experience. They are rarely involved in direct service delivery.

Administrators can be directors, principal officers, senior officers and managers. They are not to be confused with secretarial staff, who are often referred to as *administrative assistants*. These latter people are responsible for a range of office-management tasks such as typing, filing, databases and record-keeping.

Professionals and semi-professionals

The *professions* refer to certain classes of occupation which convey status. In the past, there were only three professions: medical (doctors), clerical (vicars, priests) and legal (solicitors, barristers). Over time this has changed to include a range of occupations that all have certain things in common:

- a high level of education and qualification in their field of expertise;
- adherence to a professional code of conduct;
- the need to make value judgements in their work.

Teaching, social work, health-visiting,

housing management and many other occupations are now considered professions or *semi-professions*. As the professions have grown and the roles and qualifications of staff within them have changed, a division has been made between the *professionals* and the *semi-professionals*. Semi-professionals may work in the same field but be less qualified or have a role that requires them to make fewer decisions. In the medical services, a consultant or doctor would be considered professional and the nurses, health visitors and midwives semi-professional.

Whilst this is how many organisations view the concept of 'professional', being a professional is increasingly defined by how a person does their job rather than by the status inferred by qualification.

'Professionalism'
Regardless of status, all people working in the social care arena, at whatever level, are expected to behave professionally. This means they have to adopt attitudes and behaviours consistent with their roles and responsibilities in their organisations.

activity

In small groups, cut out pictures from magazines and newspapers that in some way show what the groups think makes a person a professional, and stick them on a sheet of paper. After completing this exercise, all the groups should come together and share their ideas.

Managers

A *manager* has a general responsibility for all the functions taking place in their department or team. It is their responsibility to:

- ensure the smooth running of the service
- monitor quality control and service delivery
- supervise staff
- deal with the complaints of staff and service users
- allocate work
- allocate resources
- manage a budget
- report to others higher up the management chain or hierarchy.

All managers work in different ways. Some adopt a very authoritarian style: they dictate to the staff how they want things done; whilst others adopt a more permissive, flexible approach: they are much more likely to encourage staff to develop their own ideas and to use their own initiative.

Service providers

Service providers are responsible for the direct delivery of services to service users. They are the people who make face-to-face contact. The tasks they undertake are many and various, and they include:

- physical and tending care
- giving advice and information
- advocacy and empowerment
- observation and assessment
- investigation
- counselling and emotional support
- practical tasks, eg cooking and cleaning
- transport.

activity

Investigate the roles and responsibilities of key personnel in social care. The following chart, with one entry given, might help you to create the right layout:

Title	Component of welfare state	Service sector	Example of workplace	Client group(s)	Principal role
Nurse	Health service	Statutory Private Voluntary	NHS Trust BUPA Sue Ryder Foundation	The chronically sick and disabled, the terminally ill, hospital patients, those in residential care, the mentally ill.	To provide medical care as directed by a doctor for those who are suffering ill health or disablement.

CHAPTER 6

SOCIAL CHANGE AND POLICY CHANGE

The relationship between the institutions of the state and society as a whole creates what are called 'push' and 'pull' factors which influence the development of social policy. Political elections determine a programme of policies, but research shows that policies play only a small part in the decision of a voter over which political party to choose.

Vested interests can mean that social policies set up to solve one set of social problems can end up causing another. Some groups in society are excluded from participating in the processes which determine social policies, and their needs may not therefore be taken into account.

New social movements and **pressure groups** are means by which people can attempt to influence social policy on specific issues.

There is an increasing move to ensure user participation in the development and implementation of social policies.

The ageing population and the attendant increase in the cost of social care will be an important influencing factor in social policy in the coming decade.

Significant individuals can influence social policy.

The media too informs the way in which we develop our social values, which will in turn influence social policy.

The state and society

In modern times, we tend to consider the 'state', that is institutions such as the House of Commons, as separate from 'society', that is the population as a whole. It is generally accepted that the state acts on behalf of society in order to ensure the collective prosperity of the country. However, the relationship between the state and society is a complex one, and this chapter will consider how the various tensions between the two, often called 'push' and 'pull' factors, can influence social policy.

The idea of social control and social engineering can be helpful in understanding how social policy changes over time. What one group sees as normal behaviour can be seen as deviant by another.

The House of Commons – one institute of the 'state'

Sometimes, the values of different groups can be in direct opposition to each other.

An example: Oscar Wilde was imprisoned because he was a homosexual. In 1998, the House of Commons voted in favour of lowering the age of consent for homosexuals to 16 years, bringing it in line with the law for heterosexuals. The House of Lords blocked this legislation. This demonstrates how radically society has changed its views on the issue of homosexuality.

The study of push-and-pull factors in social policy very often involves the study of the use of power in society.

Elections

Although the broad meaning of the term 'politics' can cover any aspect of social life where there is some movement to change or sustain power relationships, the social institutions of the state are those which create or implement social policy. Political

insurance companies in the early 1970s showed that:

- 80 per cent had been to private schools
- 87 per cent had been to Oxford or Cambridge University
- 46 per cent were members of London clubs.

(This pattern is also true for Anglican bishops and High Court judges.) Women and members of the black community are very under-represented in these groups. The power that is held in British society by these groups means that decisions tend to favour their interests and exclude others.

Actions to promote social change, therefore, are usually taken on the basis of addressing issues of inequality, in other words, to challenge the current situation.

activity

Make a list of the agencies that hold power in your locality.

- What is the purpose of these agencies?

- Are they local or national?
- Do they represent the community?
- How can you influence what they do?

activity

Choose a large organisation. It could be your college or school or your local authority. Identify the people who have responsibility for decision-making in this organisation, and broadly classify them in terms of:

- age
- disability
- ethnicity
- gender.

(You may not have enough information to gain all of these for each person.)

- Is there an equal balance here?
- How do you think that these factors affect the decisions made by these people?
- What opportunities do people affected by these decisions have to challenge them?

There is clear evidence to show that a number of groups in society are disadvantaged. People from ethnic minorities, people with disabilities and women are more likely to be unemployed or to have lower terms and conditions of employment. People from ethnic minorities are disproportionately represented in the numbers of families in temporary accommodation awaiting council housing, and in the prison population. This inequality leads to the social exclusion of disadvantaged groups.

New social movements

As we have seen, in practice, elections do not always provide people with the means to influence social policy either because there are barriers to becoming involved in the political process, or because social policy is not always the overriding concern of the voters.

New social movements and pressure groups are one way in which people can attempt to influence policy on specific issues. The term 'new social movements' is used to describe groups of people who come together to campaign for social or political change. One example of a social movement is the Campaign for Nuclear Disarmament (CND) which campaigns for world peace by promoting the disarmament of all nuclear weapons. In the UK, much of the activity here has centred around protest marches in London and on nuclear bases.

Nicholas Abercrombie and Alan Warde describe new social movements as falling into different themes:

* women's equality issues
* peace
* environmental issues.

To these could also be added campaigns against racism or against discrimination against people with disabilities.

Broadly speaking, new social movements are protest movements which are speaking out against a particular established policy, and they are characterised by the fact that ordinary people feel strongly enough about the particular cause to take action. People may get involved in order to support one specific campaign, often on a local level. There is no centrally organised system; rather, the nature of actions is determined democratically by those involved. Actions can include protest marches and demonstrations, petitions and civil disobedience, and are designed to draw attention to the cause and to influence public opinion.

Pressure groups fulfil the same purpose. Research points to the fact that the more middle-class people there are involved in pressure groups, the more successful these are likely to be. Equally, however, this indicates that more marginalised groups in society, such as black people, are less likely to be listened to.

One example of a pressure group which has achieved success by pursuing social action in this way is Amnesty International. Local groups here campaign on behalf of individual political prisoners of conscience by writing letters complaining about their incarceration to key policy-makers in the countries concerned. This action has enabled prisoners to gain freedom in a number of different countries.

Some forms of action can be more direct. The riots that took place in British cities in 1981, and later in Brixton and Tottenham, are an example of how protests can be the only way in which black people can express their anger in a society that discriminates against them.

Operation Black Vote is a campaign which aims to ensure better representation of the British black community in all areas of public life by encouraging black people to participate in democracy. Currently, there are:

* 9 black MPs out of 651
* 100 black councillors
* 1 black MEP
* 5 black circuit judges
* no black High Court judges

- 1 high-ranking black police officer
- 2 black senior civil servants – grade 4 and above – out of 805.

24 per cent of the black community in Britain is not registered to vote, and according to the NOP poll in 1991, only 48 per cent of the black community were certain to vote, leaving a staggering 52 per cent of black people without a voice in British democracy. The main objectives of Operation Black Vote are:

- to enable and encourage active citizenship within the black community
- to achieve greater black political representation
- to achieve greater black representation in all areas of public life
- to ensure the concerns of the black community are high on the political agenda, both nationally and locally
- to demonstrate the benefits of black participation to society via large, peaceful black campaigns.

activity

Think of a campaign which you know about or have heard of. It could be anything from a local protest about a new road being built or a campaign for a traffic-calming system, to an international environmental issue.

- What is the campaign about?
- Who is involved?
- How is the campaign organised?
- What effect has the campaign had on social policy?

Empowerment

There has been a growing emphasis in recent years on the idea of *empowerment* in social policy. Empowerment means enabling people to have the power and resources necessary to take charge of their own lives. It is a concept which has the support of both sides of the political divide. It appeals to the political Right because it emphasises individual responsibility rather than state dependency, and it appeals to the political Left because it emphasises the process by which people are oppressed. The idea of empowerment is present, for example, in the Citizen's Charter and the Patient's Charter for Health.

Example: the Community Care (Direct Payments) Act enables people with disabilities to pay for their own services, thereby increasing their autonomy and choice. The intention of Direct Payment Schemes is to enable people with disabilities to take more control over their lives.

A Policy Studies Institute survey recommended that local authorities needed to ensure good working partnerships with organisations of people with disabilities. They make it clear that this means organisations which are controlled by people with disabilities rather than by their carers or supporters.

IMPROVING SERVICE

The Patient's Charter for Health is one initiative which embodies the notion of empowerment

Increasingly, social policy and legislation seek to ensure that the views of 'users' are consulted and taken into account. At the very minimum, most services now have to have a *complaints procedure*. Users' views have an impact on the way in which social policy is formulated and implemented.

Consultation

Consultation has become a key part of social policy. As part of legislation, Green Papers and White Papers are issued outlining proposed legislation for consultation with the main stakeholders involved. Local authorities will consult with those affected on the implementation of local schemes. Different political parties have different views about *consensus politics*, ie politics where an attempt is made to reach agreement with all concerned.

activity

1 Find out the difference between a government Green Paper and a White Paper.
2 Choose a current Paper and track its progress throughout the consultative period.

● What are the changes that have been made to the original proposal?
● Were they made as a result of consultation?
● Who do you think were the most influential people in the process, and why?

Monitoring and evaluation

Almost any piece of work which receives public funding of any kind must be monitored and evaluated, with the views of everyone involved included in order to ensure value for money. The aim of evaluation is to find out whether the piece of work met its original aims and objectives, and how these were achieved. An essential part of the evaluation process is to decide what the implications for future work and for possible policy changes might be.

activity

Most service providers now ask for consumers' views on their service, and you will probably find that your college asks for your own views on its services or on your course. Respond to a questionnaire asking for your views on a service.

● Find out what happened to your response.
● Do you think that your views were taken into account?
● Did the service change as a result of the consultation?

Funding

One of the key factors which affects the development of social policy is that of *funding*. The universalist approach to welfare adopted in the UK after the Second World War expected that the welfare state would provide for the population's basic needs. As we have seen, there has been a move towards social insurance systems, and there are limited resources with which to implement social policies.

Public expenditure on social services accounts for 40 per cent of Britain's gross domestic product (GDP), compared to 2.5 per cent at the beginning of the century. At the start of the century, social services were almost non-existent, and yet there are economic gains in providing effective social services.

Public money is raised by:

* taxation (ie on personal income and on companies and corporations, plus VAT and national insurance)
* contributions
* local taxes
* charges.

Clearly, when economic growth slows and public expenditure on social services stays the same, this causes political controversy. There have been a number of moves to cut expenditure and increase cost efficiency in the management of social services since 1976, although the expectation of service provision has remained. It is often the preventive services which are cut in these initiatives (eg broad-based family support services in favour of child protection).

Increasingly, there is an emphasis on mixed economy provision as a means of ensuring both a diversity of services to meet individual needs and efficiency. The local-authority social-services departments, for example, are moving towards becoming purchasers, rather than providers, of particular services. The Direct Payments Scheme is an example of this trend.

In the field of health, Primary Care Groups are being established to replace fundholding general practitioners as a means of ensuring that people within a locality gain the health care that they need. The Primary Care Groups will purchase services, and the intention is that this will put an end to the internal market in the National Health Service.

The reality is that with an ageing population, the cost of care will increase, and this will become a significant factor in the development of social policy. The British Social Attitudes Survey shows that there would be widespread opposition to any move to cut health spending. However, only two in five people think that people who are better off should pay for health care.

The question of resources will be a key element in the development of future social policy.

New technology

One of the factors that will affect social policy in the future is new technology. The Internet makes access to information easier, and employment patterns will almost certainly change as more people are able to work at home. This will have an effect on family and community life. Access to new technology can enable people to participate more in the development of social policy.

activity

Use your library to gain access to the Internet. Look up one of the government departments. You will be able to see any current consultation papers and recent press releases. Choose a policy you are interested in, and send your own personal direct response by e-mail to the contact named.

The influence of individuals

Individuals can play an important part in the creation of social policy. We have already mentioned earlier in this book the influence that Princess Diana had on the landmine campaign and in drawing attention to causes such as HIV and AIDS.

Members of Parliament, again as already mentioned, can also bring forward their own private member's bills and influence social policy. David Alton did this when he tried to bring in an anti-abortion bill. Administrators who are responsible for implementing social policy can also influence how this takes place depending on their personal views and beliefs.

Political parties often employ 'spin doctors' to promote a particular policy within their own party. *Non-governmental organisations (NGOs)* will employ **lobbyists** to promote their particular issues to policy-makers at national and European level.

The media

The media plays a significant role in social policy and in how we develop our social values. Soap operas are often instrumental in informing the way we think about a particular issue.

The media has played an important part in forming views about the impact of Europe on national policy. For example:

RUMOUR: Europe bans the Valentine's day card because of sexual harassment.

FACT: The European Directive on the protection of the dignity of women and men at work promotes awareness of the unacceptability of sexual harassment.

RUMOUR: Europe bans paperboys and girls.

FACT: The Protection of Young Workers Directive restricts the working hours of young people in full-time education to two hours of light work per day.

Women's fears of walking home alone at night were also said to have been fuelled by the media. In fact, young men are far more at risk of violent attacks. Equally, the stereotypical child abuser is a stranger who hangs around parks in a raincoat, when in fact it is far more likely that a child will be abused by someone who is already known to them.

Moral panics

The public is understandably concerned by some of these issues, and public concern or moral panic, whether founded or not, can have an influence on social policy. The BSE or 'Mad Cow Disease' crisis is an example of this. The World Health Organisation, the International Veterinary Organisation and the EC Scientific Committee all agreed that the measures taken by the UK government to control the spread of this disease in the food chain were sufficient and that there was no evidence of a link between the disease that affects cows, BSE (bovine spongiform encephalopathy) and CJD (Creutzfeldt-Jakob disease). Despite this, all European Union (EU) states banned British beef except for Denmark and the Republic of Ireland, as a result of public concern. The purchase of beef in the UK by consumers fell dramatically.

A wide range of factors, within a particular social context and a particular power dynamic, influence social policy change. It is necessary to understand these factors in order to understand the reasons behind the development of social policy.

CHAPTER 7

SOCIAL POLICY AND PROVISION IN THE EUROPEAN UNION

Employment issues drive social policy in the European Union (EU).

The European Community (later called the European Union) was formed on the basis of economic union. Social policy was driven by a concern to ensure that differences in social policy did not get in the way of this economic union. The European Community assumed that economic growth would improve social development.

Social policy in the EU was initially concerned with supporting migrant workers.

There has been a change of emphasis from **social harmonisation**, which aimed for a uniform approach to social policy across the EU, to an acknowledgement of the diversity of approaches, termed by Jacques Delors as **social coherence**. The goal is now for *mutual recognition*.

The EU has adopted the principle of *subsidiarity*, which means that it will only intervene where action cannot be taken at Member State level.

The **Social Charter** brings together all the fragmented parts of social policy into an overall framework.

Current priorities for the EU are the promotion of an adaptable workforce and labour markets which are responsive to economic change, together with a commitment to combat social exclusion.

There are different models of welfare in the EU, from those based on **social insurance** schemes to a **universalist** approach to welfare.

The European Structural Funds are the EU's financial instrument to support employment-related initiatives to stimulate social inclusion. The policy fields supported by the European Social Fund will be employability, entrepreneurship, adaptability and equal opportunities.

Current issues in welfare provision include the demographic trend towards an older population, the problem of youth unemployment, mutual recognition in education and training, health and safety, the protection of children, and equal opportunities between men and women. Enlargement of the EU and European Monetary Union are likely to bring about further changes in social policy.

The history of social policy in the European Union

In the European Union (EU), employment issues drive social policy. A brief look at the history of the Union demonstrates how this came about.

Table 7.1 shows the organisations, treaties and acts on which the EU is based.

The European Coal and Steel Community (ECSC) in 1951 and the European Atomic Energy Community (EURATOM, later the EAEC) in 1957 were established as a result of:

- a concern to ensure that the peoples of Europe were unified so as to avoid a repetition of the First and Second World Wars;
- an urgent need to bring together the steel and coal resources of Western Europe which had been the cause of dispute between Germany and France.

EURATOM aimed to promote international co-operation to ensure the safe and peaceful use of atomic energy.

The social-policy significance of the organisations, treaties and acts shown in Table 7.1 was the ECSC's focus on dis-placed workers from the coal and steel industries and their living and working conditions, and the EAEC's health and safety standards for workers.

The European Economic Community (EEC) was established by a treaty signed in Rome in 1957 between Belgium, France, the Federal Republic of Germany, Italy, Luxembourg and the Netherlands. The treaty aimed to create an economic union, and all references to social policy were driven by a concern to ensure that differences in social policy did not get in the way of this union by creating unfair competition between Member States. It was assumed that economic growth would improve social development. The treaty did, however:

- set up the European Social Fund (ESF) as a small-scale measure to help declining areas of the economy. The aim of the Fund was to provide help towards the geographical and occupational mobility of workers within the EEC Member States, including with the cost of vocational training and resettlement;

18/4/51	European Coal and Steel Community (ECSC)
25/3/57	European Economic Community (EEC)
25/3/57	European Atomic Energy Community (EAEC)
8/4/65	The Merger Treaty
1/7/87	Single European Act (SEA)
9/12/89	Community Charter of the Fundamental Social Rights of Workers (not UK)
1/11/93	Treaty on European Union (TEU) – Maastricht Treaty
2/10/97	Treaty of Amsterdam 1997

Table 7.1 A chronology of European legislation

- commit the EEC to raising standards of living;
- promote close co-operation between Member States in terms of social policy, particularly in areas such as employment, training and the mutual recognition of qualifications, social security and collective bargaining, working conditions and equal pay between men and women.

The ECSC, the EAEC and the EEC together formed the basis of social policy in the EU, and these three organisations were merged in 1965 to form a single Council and a single Commission of the European Communities.

EU social policy was initially concerned with:

- freedom of movement of workers
- giving help to migrant workers.

In particular, the Treaty of Rome wanted to ensure that no one Member State would be at a competitive advantage or disadvantage as a result of its social policies. Article 117 of this Treaty anticipated that the Common Market would 'favour the harmonisation of social systems'.

From the beginning, social policy was always determined by individual Member States, with the EEC treaty promoting the idea of *approximation*, meaning that there should be a broadly similar approach to social systems in each state. This was left to the individual states to achieve, and the treaty was only prescriptive in the case of social-security arrangements for migrant workers.

The idea of harmonisation of social protection was that Member States should use their national legal system to ensure a uniform approach across the EU. However, since 1957, there has been a change of emphasis regarding the harmonisation of social policy in Europe as doubts have

been raised over the feasibility or even desirability of this goal (Hantrais, 1997). Some of the debate about harmonisation has been influenced by new Member States at different times, and this will no doubt continue as more European countries apply for membership of the EU.

Some of the concerns of Member States centre around two issues:

- 'social dumping' whereby companies relocate their business to countries in which the labour and social costs are cheaper;
- 'welfare or social tourism' where workers and the unemployed might wish to relocate to Member States with more generous welfare systems.

In 1985, when Jacques Delors became President of the Commission, he advocated the goal of *coherence*, meaning that the European Community should aim to work together in some kind of consistent and orderly way. This represented a change in emphasis from the meaning of harmonisation as uniformity, or being the same, which would have been opposed by Member States who did not wish to change their national systems, and a move towards a respect for the differences in national systems. Delors advocated social dialogue between unions and employers as the means to achieve **social coherence**, with the European Commission taking a more facilitative role.

This shift in thinking is reflected in both the Single European Act 1987 and the Community Charter of the Fundamental Social Rights of Workers 1989, otherwise known as the Social Charter, where harmonisation is still mentioned but now in the context of recognition for differences in national systems. The aim now was not to try and change social systems of Member States but to encourage them to: 'converge over a number of precisely

EEC founder members:

Belgium (10m inhabitants)

France (57m inhabitants)

Germany (81m inhabitants)

Italy (58m inhabitants)

Luxembourg (under 400,000 inhabitants)

The Netherlands (15m inhabitants)

Joined in 1972:

Denmark (5m inhabitants)

Ireland (3.5m inhabitants)

United Kingdom (58m inhabitants)

Joined in the 1980s:

1981 Greece (10m inhabitants)

1986 Portugal (10m inhabitants)

1986 Spain (39m inhabitants)

Joined in 1995:

Austria (8m inhabitants)

Finland (5m inhabitants)

Sweden (9m inhabitants)

Applications to join the EU (accession):

1987 Turkey

1990 Cyprus

1991 Liechtenstein

1994 Hungary and Poland

1995 Latvia, Slovakia, Estonia, Bulgaria and Lithuania

1996 The Czech Republic and Slovenia

Applications for accession under agenda 2000:

Bulgaria	Lithuania
The Czech Republic	Poland
Estonia	Romania
Hungary	Slovakia
Latvia	Slovenia

Table 7.2 European Union membership

defined common objectives without encroaching on systems which have developed from quite different traditions' (Hantrais, 1997).

The fears of Member States regarding the implications of **social harmonisation** can be illustrated by the UK, which did not sign up to the **Social Charter**. There were two reasons for this: first, the fear that majority Community decisions regarding employment and social policy would force change on UK systems; and second, a concern that the Social Charter would create raised costs for employers, increased job losses and a reduction in competitiveness. In order to combat this kind of concern on the part of Member States, the principle of *subsidiarity* was adopted. This meant that the EU would only intervene where necessary and where action could not be taken at a national level to achieve its common objectives.

The Maastricht Treaty emphasised the importance of social cohesion as the means of promoting sustainable economic and social progress. The terms 'approximation' and 'harmonisation' do not appear in the Social Chapter, which is annexed to the Maastricht Treaty as the

Agreement on Social Policy, and Member States are encouraged to promote 'proper social protection' whilst taking into account 'diverse forms of national practices' (Article 1).

THE SOCIAL CHARTER

The Social Charter is an agreement which was adopted by 11 Member States except for the UK in 1989. It contains 47 initiatives and brings together all the fragmented parts of social policy into an overall framework. Areas covered by the Social Charter include the following:

- living and working conditions;
- freedom of movement of workers, including equal treatment and the right to exercise any occupation and receive the same social protection as nationals of the host state;
- a fair wage in all employment;
- social protection and a minimum income for the unemployed;
- trade-union membership and worker participation;
- vocational training throughout working life;
- equal treatment between men and women;
- health and safety in the workplace;
- child protection (a minimum working age of 16);
- a minimum income for elderly people;
- the integration of people with disabilities into working life.

THE 1994 WHITE PAPER ON EUROPEAN SOCIAL POLICY

This White Paper outlined a strategy which aimed to combat the social exclusion of disadvantaged groups and to tackle poverty in the EU. In 1994, all Member States of the EU except for the UK adopted a resolution on European social policy which outlined its aims as follows:

- to increase the competitiveness of the EU and increase its chances of job-generating growth;
- to protect workers' rights through minimum social standards;
- to respect the principle of subsidiarity;
- to aim for the convergence of social systems rather than making them uniform;
- to agree on specific social and economic measures.

THE AMSTERDAM TREATY 1997

This Treaty ended the UK opt-out on the Social Charter and strengthened the provisions of the Charter itself. It inserted a new section on employment, with the stated principle that: 'Member States shall work towards a co-ordinated strategy for employment and the promotion of a skilled, trained and adaptable workforce and labour markets responsive to economic change.' Member States now have to draw up annual employment action plans. The evaluation of these will form the basis for action taken by the European Council.

A new provision was made to combat social exclusion, and allows for a continuation of anti-poverty programmes. In addition, the Treaty states that the Commission must promote and support the social dialogue between unions and employers.

Models of welfare

There are clear differences between the different models of welfare in different EU Member States. As well as fundamental differences in approach to social welfare, each country has its own history of social-welfare development and structural differences in provision which explain the difficulties involved in achieving social harmonisation.

The funding of social welfare systems varies greatly across the Union, with Denmark and Ireland depending heavily on state subsidies, France, Italy and Spain on employers' contributions, and the Netherlands on the contributions of employees.

Linda Hantrais (1997) distinguishes between three broad models of welfare in Europe. These models are known as the Continental, Nordic and Anglo-Saxon and Southern European.

CONTINENTAL WELFARE STATES

This model is shared by the founder members of the EEC and works on the basis that individuals qualify for benefits through **social insurance** schemes which are linked to employment. Benefits are mostly funded through employer and employee contributions. This is most like Titmuss's *individual and industrial achievement models*, and unfortunately, there are inherent inequalities in the system which discriminates against groups known to be disadvantaged in the labour market, such as young people, ethnic-minority groups and women.

Social protection schemes here cover, in order of priority, industrial injury and occupational diseases, sickness and maternity benefits, old-age, survivors' and invalidity benefits, unemployment benefits and family allowances.

Most health-care provision here is also based on insurance contributions, with the exception of Italy which has a National Health Service. All six founder members have some form of non-contributory social security as a safety net, financed through general taxation. Their spending on social welfare is generally higher than in other Member States.

However, all six states are very different in terms of funding arrangements and organisation of provision, and where there is regional organisation, there are also significant differences within states. The differences between northern and southern Italy illustrate this.

NORDIC AND ANGLO-SAXON WELFARE STATES

Denmark, Ireland and the UK all joined the Community in 1973 and shared a model of welfare that was based on the precept that all citizens were entitled to social assistance regardless of employment status. This equates to Titmuss's *universal model of welfare*.

Social-security systems are funded by general taxation, and health-care provision is universal rather than dependent on social insurance systems. The Danish system emphasises income maintenance whilst the UK and Ireland provide low flat-rate payments or means-tested social assistance, which accounts for the differences in state spending levels between these Member States.

THE SOUTHERN EUROPEAN WELFARE MODEL

Greece, Portugal and Spain joined the EU in the 1980s, and rely on the family and the Church to provide social protection. Health provision in Spain and Portugal is provided by the state through taxation, and other forms of social assistance are provided through employer contributions. By the early 1990s, many people were still not covered by social insurance, and there was no general social assistance scheme in Greece and Portugal. In contrast to the other Member States, expenditure on social protection has increased significantly in these countries.

However, significant changes have taken place in social welfare over the post-war period which have led to a convergence of sorts. In particular, there has been a move towards a mixed economy approach to social welfare, with the development of social insurance schemes. In the UK, for example, private health-care and occupational schemes are increasing. On the other hand, countries with employment-related insurance schemes, such as France and Belgium, have developed social assistance schemes for older people who are not eligible for employment-related schemes.

(Pages 119–120 adapted from Hantrais, 1997.)

The overall trend towards employment insurance in social welfare raises the issue of social exclusion, however, as it reinforces the marginalisation of groups that are disadvantaged in the workforce. The EU has increasingly focused on this area through its Structural Funds.

European Structural Funds

The European Structural Funds are the EU's financial instrument for supporting employment-related initiatives to stimulate social and economic regeneration. The Structural Funds are made up of:

- The European Regional Development Fund (ERDF): to assist the growth, adjustment and redevelopment of regional economies affected by industrial decline or structural deficits;
- The European Social Fund (ESF): founded in 1960 to improve employment opportunities by providing support for vocational training schemes and job-creation measures;
- The European Agricultural Guidance and Guarantee Fund (EAGGF): established in 1962 to assist countries with the modernisation of agricultural infrastructures, and to support farming in environmentally sensitive areas.

In the period 1994–99, the priorities for the European Social Fund were those of:

- combating long-term unemployment and assisting young people into work;
- helping those exposed to exclusion from the labour market;
- promoting equal opportunities for men and women;
- providing support for workers having to adapt to industrial change.

The draft regulations for the seven-year period 2000–2006 have been developed around the following principles:

- the need for greater cost-effectiveness;
- the desire for a new partnership between the Commission and the Member States which gives a wider remit to the individual Member State;
- the promotion of four basic Community priorities:
  1 sustainable economic development
  2 competitiveness and innovation
  3 employment and human resources
  4 equality of opportunity between men and women.

The Funds will be targeted on regions whose development is lagging behind, on regions undergoing economic and social conversion, and on the development of human resources. In addition, 5 per cent of the total Structural Funds budget of ECU 210 billion will be made available for transnational Community Initiatives to stimulate Member States, regions and economic and social partners to work together in areas of common interest to the EU.

The general policy fields of the European Social Fund post-2000 will be:

- employability
- entrepreneurship
- adaptability
- equal opportunities.

These are the same priorities as can be found in the European Economic Strategy and the Title of Employment in the Treaty of Amsterdam 1997.

The Structural Funds post-2000 have made a significant shift towards the promotion of social inclusion and equal opportunities in the labour market. Initiatives will focus specifically on life-long learning (enabling people to continue training throughout their lives) as a means of enabling Europe's population to adapt to the changing needs of the workforce.

activity

Find out if there are any European Social Fund projects operating in your region (contact your European Officer, local authority or government office for this information). If so:

- What does the project do?
- How does it fit into the European Structural Funds objectives?

How European social policy is made, and the extent of its powers

There are four main EC institutions.

1 The *Council of Ministers* (now called the *Council of the European Union*). This is made up of representatives of governments of the 15 Member States; different Ministers attend depending on the topics under discussion.

2 The *European Commission*. This is the civil service of the EU, and it has 24

CASE STUDY

Provision and practice: European childcare

We have seen how different European countries have very different approaches to social welfare, shaped by their cultures and histories. A study of childcare across five Member States demonstrates how different provision can occur in the EU. There are significant differences both in state funding and in the organisation of provision, as well as in administrative arrangements and statutory require-ments. Table 7.3 gives a snapshot of the differences and similarities in the field of childcare.

Table 7.4 looks at the qualifacatory requirements for working with children. These too reveal significant differences, and demonstrate why it is no easy task to hold a qualification which would equip someone to work in all EU countries.

Both these tables were prepared by the REA transnational partnership: Reggio Children in Reggio Emilia in Italy, Association Relais in Nancy, France, and the HERA 2 Project in the UK; as part of a European Social Fund project: New Opportunities for Women.

Directorates General, known as 'DG' followed by the number, in Roman numerals, of the directorate. For exam-ple, DGV deals with employment, industrial relations and social affairs, DGXXII with education, training and youth, and DGXXIV with consumer and health-protection policy.

3 The *European Parliament*. This now has 626 members, and can call on the Commission to prepare legislation. It has the power to dismiss the Commission, and the right to be con-sulted on Commission proposals and make amendments where appropriate. These are then referred to the Council of Ministers.

4 The *Court of Justice*. This carries out judicial supervision of the treaties and Community legislation. Its role is to enforce Community legislation.

These institutions are supported by:

- The *Court of Auditors* which monitors the Community's budget;
- The *Committee of the Regions* which is made up of representatives of local and regional authorities. It is consulted on regional policies, economic and social cohesion, trans-European networks, education, vocational training, public health and cultural policies;
- The *Economic and Social Committee* which is made up of representatives of trade unions and professional bodies and gives its opinion on Commission proposals;
- The *Committee of Representatives (COREPER)* which prepares work for the Council of Ministers.

The European Council consists of govern-ment heads of state of Member States,

	France	Italy	UK	Denmark	Spain
History	Long tradition of public-sector early-childhood education.	Public funding for 3–6-year-olds from 1968 when Ministry of Education took responsibility for kindergartens.	Diverse, fragmented system left to the market to provide, until 1998 when co-ordinated through local partnerships.	An integrated system.	Reorganisation of services from 1990, recognising education for children 0–3 and children 3–6.
State subsidy	Tax benefits for families subsidise childcare. Nurseries and family daycare funded by parental contributions, regional family allowances and local authorities.	Attendance at state-run centres for children 3–6 is free; parents pay income-related contributions to local authority centres. Parents pay 36% of costs for *asili nidi* (0–3-year-olds).	Only for children in need, until 1997/98 when tax benefits for families brought in, plus grants to encourage development of new places, funding for education of 4-year-olds (see Chapter 8).	Parents contribute a fifth of the costs, the rest is funded by the state.	There is income-related tax relief for parents.
Children under 3	20% of children under 3 attend private, public or voluntary provision.	Low levels of provision, no organised provision, mainly family daycare or family members.	1–2% of children attend publicly funded provision. Majority of provision in family daycare.	55% of children attend publicly funded services, family daycare, nurseries for children 0–3 or age-integrated provision for 0–6 and over.	20–30% attend a centre, but only 5% attend a publicly funded centre. Family daycare is rare.
Children 3–6	Legal entitlement to place in *école maternelle* provides education for most 3–6-year-olds. A variety of other statutory, voluntary and private-sector provision. Over a third of 2-year-olds also attend an *école maternelle*.	92% of children between 3 and 6 years attend provision (*scuola materna*), although the north is better provided for than the south	53% of children attend publicly funded provision. Nursery places available for just over a quarter of 3- and 4-year-olds in 1996. All 4-year-olds have access to free education from September 1998. Playgroups are a significant provider.	88% of children attend publicly funded services in centres for 3–6-year-olds or age-integrated.	84% of children in 1993/94 attended services, and nearly all 4- and 5-year-olds.
Statutory school age	6.	6.	5 (4 in Northern Ireland).	7.	6.
Out-of-school	Wrap-around provision for all children.	Very few services.	Out-of-school clubs increasing through recent government policy.		
Administration	Ministry of Education: *école maternelle*; Ministry of Social Affairs: children under 3; Ministry of Youth and Sport: out-of-school activities.	Ministry of Education: children 3–6; Ministry of Health: children under 3.	Department of Education and Employment: schools and regulation; Department of Health: children in need.	Ministry of Social Affairs is responsible for integrated services for children under statutory school age. Standards are set locally within a decentralised system.	Ministry of Education: the 0–6 age group has a national curriculum and national standards.
Women's employment	59% women with children under 10 are employed full-time. 14% part-time.	43% of women with children under 10 are employed.	53% of mothers with children under 10 are employed, mostly part-time.	80% of women have full-time employment.	One of the lowest levels of maternal employment in Europe.

Source: REA transnational partnership: *New Opportunities for Women.*

Table 7.3   European models of childcare

	France	Italy	UK	Denmark	Spain
Teacher	Baccalauréat plus years at university. Employment in école maternelle and primary school. Training covers ages 2–11.	8 years of school (until age 14) plus teacher training college (5 years). Employment in primary school and scuola materna.	12 years of schooling plus 5 GCSEs including English, Maths and Science plus 2 A levels plus 3–4 years at university. Employment in local authority nursery, primary school.	Pedagogue training (social educator) in specialised colleges. Minimum age 18, but average age 27. College admission criteria give priority to work experience.	Minimum age 18. Degree in Early-childhood Teaching specialising in work with children 0–6 years.
Nursery worker	Baccalauréat plus 2-year training in social or paramedical profession or qualification as a health visitor or health-visitor assistant. Employment in nursery for 0–2s, parent co-operative nursery for 0–4s, kindergarten for 2–6 years, sessional daycare 6 months to 6 years.	8 years of school (to 14 years) plus 3 years at scuola magistrale or 5 years on vocational training scheme (entitles university entrance). Employment in scuola materna and asilo nido. Assistant can undertake a 3-year assistant training programme. Assistants in asili nidi undertake courses of between 6 months and 1 year. Courses are not nationally recognised.	Completion of compulsory schooling (age 16) plus 2-year full-time or part-time routes with experience to level-3 qualification (pre-university).	As above.	As above. Minimum age 18. 2,000 hours of training, of which 400 hours involve practical work in centres. Employment as senior worker in childhood education for children 0–3 years.
Playworker	Minimum age 17. Ministry of Youth and Sport-recognised training courses of 160 hours with 4–8-month placements.	6-month to 2-year courses. Courses are not nationally recognised.	Variety of playwork courses, with different recognition levels, across the UK.	As above.	
Family daycare	60 hours in the first year.	None.	Varies. Pre-registration courses 4–20 hours. Regulation involved.	Pedagogical basic training for 1 to 1½ years depending on experience.	

Source: REA transnational partnership: New Opportunities for Women.

Table 7.4   Training required to work with children in the European Union

their Ministers for Foreign Affairs and the President of the European Commission. It meets twice a year to discuss major political issues and policies. The President of the European Commission briefs the European Parliament on the conclusions of each meeting. The Presidency of the EU rotates every six months.

The largest Member States – France, Germany, Italy and the UK – have 10 votes each, Spain has 8 votes, Belgium, Greece, the Netherlands and Portugal have 5 votes, Austria and Sweden have 4 votes, Denmark, Finland and Ireland have 3 votes and Luxembourg has 2 votes.

European Community law has priority over any conflicting law in Member States. National courts must interpret national laws in the context of Community legislation.

European law or policy is established in the following ways.

PRIMARY LEGISLATION

Primary legislation comprises international acts, treaties and agreements that amend or adapt former treaties. Examples include the Treaty of Rome 1957, the Merger Treaty of 1965, the Single European Act of 1986, the Treaty on European Union of 1992 and the Treaty of Amsterdam 1997.

SECONDARY LEGISLATION

Secondary legislation comprises acts passed to ensure that the treaties establishing the communities are applied.

- *Regulations:* these are directly enforceable laws which are binding in Member States.
- *Directives:* these are legally binding, and lay down the intended results of legisla-

tion. It is up to Member States to achieve these aims within the time limit.
- *Decisions:* these are addressed to Member States, to a company, or to an individual, and are legally binding on the addressee.
- *Recommendations and opinions:* these are not legally binding but have significant political influence.
- *Notices:* these are intended to provide guidance.
- *Inter-institutional agreements:* these enable the Council, Parliament and Commission to implement decisions set out in the treaties.
- *Conventions:* These are not Community law, but they are effective where they have been agreed by Member States.
- *Agreements:* these are made between the EU and other countries.

With the exception of issues concerning the free movement of labour and the Structural Funds, the EU has used very few **regulations**.

PASSING LEGISLATION

The procedure for passing legislation depends on the Article of the Treaty under which the proposal is brought forward. The procedures vary according to the legislation, but they involve consultation between the Commission, the Council and the Parliament, and use the advisory bodies such as the Committee of the Regions where appropriate. Some of the procedures vary according both to timescales set for the consideration of proposed legislation at each stage, and to the degree of unanimity necessary for proposals to be agreed at each stage.

Figure 7.1 gives an example of the most simple of the procedures used to pass legislation: the consultation procedure.

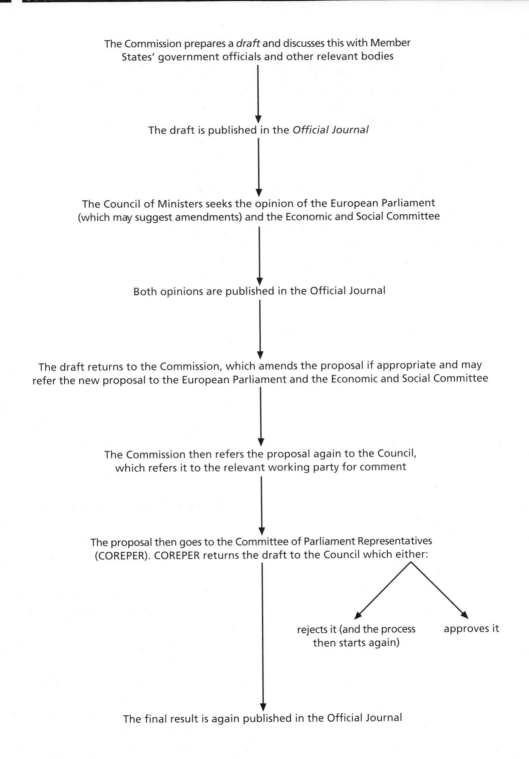

Figure 7.1   The consultation procedure

activity

Find out your local representative on the   European Member of Parliament.
Committee of the Regions and your local

activity

Find out if there are any Directives which   Have they affected any organisations or
have had an impact on UK legislation.   individuals locally?

Current issues in welfare provision

AN AGEING POPULATION

A study of demographic trends in Europe
shows that over the next 30 years the
population aged over 60 could grow by 50
per cent. At the same time, the number of
young people between 0 and 19 will fall
by 11 per cent, and adults between 20 and
59 years will fall by 6 per cent.

The effects of an ageing population are
already being felt in the field of social
welfare, particularly with regard to retirement pensions and health. There will be
an increasing burden on social protection
to deal with the increase in older people.
This is likely to be exacerbated by the fact
that there will be a smaller working population to contribute to funding in this area.

There will be an increasing need to
ensure that the population of working age
is active in the labour market. This will
require policies which ensure that groups,
particularly women and the working age
population over 55, who are often

excluded from the labour market are
encouraged to participate.

There will also be an increasingly older
workforce. In the past, the workforce has
been able to renew skills by the flow of
young people into employment. This will
no longer be possible, and the workforce
will need to have access to skills training
and retraining through lifelong learning
measures and greater flexibility of terms
and conditions of employment in order to
ensure productivity and motivation.

Whilst there is a general trend towards
an older population, there will be important regional differences in this pattern,
with populations in some regions ageing
faster. This may mean that there is greater
geographical mobility of the workforce to
meet labour-market demands. Some
regions will face greater costs in terms of
housing, health and care needs.

Many Member States are looking at a
range of methods, in particular the development of mixed economy social welfare

and social insurance schemes, in order to prepare for the increased demands of elder care.

YOUTH UNEMPLOYMENT

There is a general concern in Europe about the current levels of unemployment of young people. The average rate here is 20.9 per cent, compared to 10.7 per cent for the whole population. Recent studies show that youth unemployment is increasing, and that 18 regions have rates of over 40 per cent. The additional need to create an adaptable, multi-skilled and mobile workforce, to meet the changing needs of the labour market, has focused attention on youth training programmes – many of which have been funded through the European Social Fund.

EDUCATION AND TRAINING

The EU has attempted to work towards the mutual recognition of qualifications between Member States, with over 60 Directives being adopted since 1964, covering sectors such as personal services, bars and hotels, restaurants, food industries and insurance agents, as well as the medical profession, accountants, lawyers and architects. It took 17 years to negotiate the right for architects to work in other Member States, and many professionals are forced to fulfil the requirements of the individual Member States, undertaking further tests or diplomas before being able to practise.

There is a trend for young people to remain in education for longer in Europe. However, there are great differences in compulsory school ages between different Member States. Children start school at age 5 in some Member States (namely the UK, Belgium, Luxembourg and the Netherlands), at age 6 in all other Member States, but at age 7 in Denmark. However, in some Member States, most children start their schooling in pre-school establishments from 3 years of age.

In Italy and Spain, children can leave school at age 14, which does not meet the Community Charter which lays down 15 as the minimum age for leaving school. In some Member States, children can leave school at 15, in others at 16.

activity

What is your chosen career? Find out if your qualifications would be recognised in other European countries. Would you be able to work in the rest of Europe? Are there any barriers which you would have to consider?

HEALTH AND SAFETY

There are about 10 million victims of accidents or occupational diseases (ie illnesses occurring as a result of employment) in the EU every year, and an estimated 6,000 people a year die from these.

A range of Directives on health and

safety have been passed, which include the following issues:

- manual handling (lifting)
- risk assessment

- first aid
- safety training
- accident and disease records
- display-screen equipment (computers).

activity

Choose one of the above, and find out your college's or employer's policy in your chosen area.

- How does it link to national legislation?
- How does it link to European Directives in your chosen area?

HEALTH

The role of the European Community is to support the work of Member States in the field of public health to ensure health protection across the whole of the EU. The European Commission is concerned with health promotion and health monitoring across the EU, and targets particular areas, including currently:

- cancer
- drug dependence
- AIDS and other transmissible diseases.

Life expectancy at birth has risen by five years since 1970, but the European Commission's report on public health in the European Community in April 1998 pointed to serious health problems, including the following:

- One in five people dies prematurely from avoidable diseases linked to lifestyle or as a result of accidents.
- New risks to health are emerging, especially from transmissible diseases.
- There are still wide differences in health depending on social class.
- There is a substantial increase in diseases related to old age, such as

Alzheimer's disease, due to the ageing population.

Health-care systems across the EU are spending more on health care partly as a result of new medical technology and of increased expectations from the public, but at the same time there is a need to ensure their cost-effectiveness without losing sight of the economic importance of a healthy population.

There are substantial differences between the health-care systems of existing Member States and those of countries in central and eastern Europe. With enlargement, the EU will need to help new countries coming into the EU to improve their health-care systems.

At the time of writing, the European Commission is proposing three new strands of action in the health field:

1 improving information for the development of public health;
2 reacting rapidly to threats to health;
3 increasing health promotion and disease prevention.

THE PROTECTION OF CHILDREN

At least 1.5 million children over 15 work outside school hours in the EU. The protection of children was included in the Social Charter, and the 1994 Council Directive on the Protection of Young People set minimum health and safety standards for young people at work. These standards include:

- a minimum working age of 16;
- a limit of 12 hours' employment per week and 2 hours per day for young people under 18 in full-time education;
- provisions such as insurance, specified rest periods and night work.

Other areas under discussion include:

- the sexual exploitation of children;
- protection of children from pornography through a variety of media;
- the European Charter of Children's Rights;
- the Convention of the Hague on the Protection of Minors.

EQUAL OPPORTUNITIES BETWEEN MEN AND WOMEN

This area has been given priority in the EU over a number of years, and is reflected in a number of Directives:

- The Directive of Equal Pay of 1975 ensured that men and women were given equal pay for work of equal value.

  Example: in 1981, a canteen cook claimed that her work was of equal value to that of a tradesman who worked in the same company. She took the case to the European Court of Justice and was awarded a pay rise.
- The European Court of Justice has established that women have the right to retire at the same age as the men with whom they work, and further Directives have ensured that private company pensions are paid to men and women at the same age.
- The Parental Leave Directive was adopted under the Social Charter, and will ensure, from 1998, that workers of both sexes are given three months' unpaid leave to care for children under the age of eight, and will also be given time off in case of family sickness or accident.
- The Part-Time Workers Directive (mainly affecting women) will give part-time workers the right to equal treatment with their full-time colleagues.

Four Community action programmes have played an important role in improving the situation for women in employment. The Community Initiative Employment NOW (New Opportunities for Women) programme has also enabled the development of a range of initiatives to facilitate access to employment for women.

Campaigning in Europe

There are a range of European-wide organisations which promote areas of social policy at European levels. These include:

- the European Disability Forum
- the Women's Lobby
- the European Local Authorities Interactive Network on Ethnic Minorities (ELAINE).

In conclusion, European social policy is closely linked with employment policy. The main preoccupation at the time of writing is to:

- encourage growth
- reduce unemployment
- train an adaptable workforce in order to keep the EU competitive.

The enlargement of the Union and European Monetary Union are both likely to bring about further changes in social policy.

CHAPTER 8

CURRENT ISSUES AND CONTROVERSIES IN SOCIAL POLICY

It is the nature of social policy and social change that new issues and controversies emerge all the time. The current Labour government, which came into power in 1997, is implementing a raft of new social policies based on linking welfare reform to employment. There is also a growing emphasis on social insurance schemes to meet the needs of the ageing population. Education is also a key priority for the current government, with a range of policies enacted to improve the education and training standards of the whole population. Health and Social Services will be modernised over the next few years, with an increased emphasis on partnership working and user involvement. Housing finance will be rationalised, and local authorities are separating their strategic role from their provider role.

The government is putting into place measures to reduce discrimination against people with disabilities and ensure that they gain access to work, and to reduce spending on Incapacity Benefit systems which support families and children, as well as tackling child poverty. Social exclusion is also a key priority, and initiatives tackling housing estates, truancy and rough sleeping involve cross-government working in order to achieve success. There are plans to improve fraud detection, particularly with respect to Housing Benefit.

There is also an increased emphasis on partnership working, customer satisfaction and user involvement, which runs across all new social policy. The co-ordination of the work of government departments with that of other agencies to ensure a joint approach has been termed by the Labour government as 'joined-up thinking'.

Changes are being implemented in the fields of mental health and children in the care system. There is also a growing awareness of environmental issues and of the need for policies to ensure **sustainability**.

The new Regional Development Agency or RDA is aimed at promoting sustainable economic development and social and physical regeneration. The current government also believes that local authorities should be more in touch with people and provide the vision for local communities, and is introducing local government reforms to meet these aims. **Devolution**, with its aim of giving real responsibility over local affairs to those living in the nation or region concerned, is also a significant force in policy development.

Readers should refer to Chapter 9 for the activities which relate to policy discussed in this chapter.

Welfare reform

The current government has linked welfare reform to employment under the Welfare to Work initiative, and its maxim is: 'Work for those who can; security for those who cannot.' There is a concern that the gap between high and low earners has widened and that the number of 'workless' households in which no one has a job has grown. There are more older people, more single parents and more divorce and separation. The government's vision for the year 2020 is that:

> There will be a new welfare 'contract', which will deliver greater trust, transparency, responsiveness and responsibility. Welfare will be provided by our Active Modern Service, based on a work-focused agency (for those seeking work); mutuals and private providers, delivering a substantial share of welfare provision, particularly pensions; and high-quality health, education and other welfare services.
>
> (DfEE, 1998)

What follows outlines the basic principles of the government's current welfare reform programme. Individual areas will be explored in more detail later on in the chapter.

WORK

One in five working-age households have no one in work, and there is high youth unemployment. The current thinking is that work is the way to help people out of poverty, and the following policies are being put into place in order to facilitate this aim:

- the New Deal which targets young people, lone parents, the long-term unemployed and people with a disability or long-term illness;
- Working Families Tax Credit which aims to offer more support to working families;
- reform of the tax and benefits system;
- a national minimum wage;
- modernisation of the national insurance scheme;
- access to childcare.

The aim of these policies is to support people to take up employment opportunities and to remove any financial disincentives to work. Through the measures listed above, the government hopes to:

- reduce the number of people of working age living in workless households;
- reduce the number of people of working age out of work for more than two years;
- increase the number of working-age people in work;
- increase the number of lone parents, people with a long-term illness, and disabled people of working age, in touch with the labour market.

SOCIAL INSURANCE

The public and private sectors are being encouraged to work in partnership to ensure that people are insured against risks and make provision for their retirement. The government's proposals in this area include:

- Stakeholder Pensions to give wider access to a second pension
- Citizenship Pensions

labour market. The British Social Attitudes Survey shows that employees are worried about job security:

- Only 55 per cent of employees believe they would have any say in decisions at work which might change their jobs, compared to 62 per cent in 1985.
- 45 per cent believe that the gap between the highest paid and the lowest paid at work is too large, compared to 40 per cent in 1985.
- 46 per cent would like more say in work decisions, compared to 36 per cent in 1985.
- Employees now want unions to protect existing jobs as a top priority, whereas eight years ago, the priority was to improve pay and/or working conditions.

Flexible employment opportunities have often been the way in which unemployed people get back to work, and they have won support in some areas for the way in which they enable women to juggle family responsibilities with work. However, the Policy Studies Institute, conducting research with a national sample of over 850 people who were unemployed in 1990–92, found that 75 per cent of the jobs they took were temporary, part-time, self-employed or at a lower skills level than their previous employment. Following the sample through to 1995, they discovered that:

- a fifth of the sample were still unemployed;
- those who had become self-employed remained so;
- there was little evidence of upward mobility;
- 25 per cent remained on temporary contracts;
- women with young children, single people and older men experienced particular difficulties in gaining employment;
- families had even lost out financially where women had taken temporary work and where either women or men had moved into part-time work.

There is a debate about whether a flexible job market really does improve employment opportunities and combat unemployment, or whether it creates a more flexible workforce, which is more in the interests of employers rather than employees. The idea of entrepreneurship is being backed by Europe and the current UK government as a means of developing new jobs. There is backing for business support through the European Structural Funds and the Training and Enterprise Councils. Many young people, in a recent survey, said that their aim was to run their own business.

New policies in this area such as the European Directive for Part-Time Workers, due to be implemented in the UK in 1999, should ensure that part-time workers receive treatment comparable to full-time workers in terms of working conditions. The Minimum Wage will make an impact on the lowest-paid jobs, although self-employment falls outside its remit.

Social policy over the last 20 years has sought, by different means, to tackle social exclusion through combating unemployment. The Conservative governments since 1979 have campaigned against welfare dependency, believing that a generous system of welfare benefits makes people less willing to look after themselves.

The British Social Attitudes Survey shows that no more than 28 per cent of its sample believe that too many 'undeserving' people get social-security benefits. The research shows that, in the main, the unemployed are just as committed to work as those in employment.

The current Labour government's New Deal programme tackles unemployment amongst young, long-term unemployed and lone parents

The notion of using employment as the means of tackling the welfare bill has been taken up by the Labour government in its Welfare to Work policies. These aim to enable those people who are disadvantaged in the labour market to gain employment.

The New Deal programme targets:

- young unemployed people between 18 and 24 years, aiming to improve their employability through work experience and training;
- older workers over 25 who are long-term unemployed;
- lone parents.

CASE STUDY

Lone Parents

The issue of lone parents is a very significant one currently because of the increase in this group all over Europe, but particularly in the UK where there is a very high percentage of lone-parent families.

The Policy Studies Institute's research into lone parenthood shows the clear link between lone parents and poverty. Single women who are poor are more likely to become lone parents, whilst separated mothers are likely to experience a decline in incomes and living standards following separation.

A separate study of illness and disability amongst lone-parent families between 1991 and 1995 showed a significant increase (14 per cent) in long-term or limiting illness of the parent, with the proportion of families with ill children also increasing by 16 per cent. Illness was also reported as a barrier to employment. The researchers concluded that although employment and maintenance from the Child Support Agency had helped some families, the New Deal for Lone Parents should improve the situation, but they indicated that 'Welfare-to-work will have to wait for welfare-to-health' (Dr Alan Marsh, Policy Studies Institute).

Social exclusion

The current Labour government has set up a Social Exclusion Unit under the Cabinet Office in an attempt to tackle what David Blunkett, Secretary of State for Education and Employment, called 'the cost of social exclusion to the communities affected as well as to welfare budgets'. Social exclusion has been linked to crime, ill health, welfare dependency, social breakdown and dislocation. Priorities for the Social Exclusion Unit include:

- truancy and school exclusion
- rough sleeping
- the worst housing estates.

The Unit hopes to tackle these and other issues by co-ordinating the work of government departments with that of other agencies to ensure a joint approach. This approach, as already mentioned, the Labour government has termed 'joined-up thinking'.

One of the initiatives to tackle social exclusion is the New Deal for Communities, a new fund worth £800 million over three years to help turn round the poorest neighbourhoods. The Social Exclusion Unit has shown that these areas have severe 'joined-up' problems, usually including:

- poor job prospects
- high levels of crime
- a run-down environment
- no one in charge of managing the neighbourhood and co-ordinating the public services that affect it.

The aim of the new programme is to support plans that bring together local people, community and voluntary organisations, public agencies, local authorities and business, in an intensive local focus to tackle these problems and make a lasting improvement.

The social-exclusion policies are designed to help solve the multiplicity of problems faced both by lone parents (see the case study) and by other groups facing additional disadvantage, by enabling government departments to work together to address these issues:

> Tackling social exclusion also requires government to work in new ways. We need to reinvent government if we are going to transform the culture in disadvantaged communities and bring about radical changes in the life chances of individuals and families. We need to rethink fundamentally how we develop and deliver social policies on a multi-agency, multi-faceted basis, and how we work with local organisations and partnerships to tackle multiple disadvantage. ... Social and economic progress need to go hand-in-hand. If one or the other is neglected the result will be instability and injustice – as well as a waste of precious human resources. Modernisation with security is the only way forward, but no society can survive and prosper if it marginalises or excludes a minority of its citizens.
>
> David Blunkett, President of the Social Affairs Council of the European Parliament, in a speech to the Social Policy Forum, June 1998 (DfEE, 329/38)

The family

Social policies concerning the family have been the subject of controversy over the past few years. As already mentioned, the Conservative view, as expressed by the independent Centre-Right think tank, is that the family is a private institution which should not be the subject of social policy, whilst the current Labour government, on the other hand, has implemented a series of social policies which impact on the family. Legislating for the family is always a controversial area. Some people resent the intrusion into what they consider to be their private and personal lives and see family legislation as an example of the 'nanny state', whilst others welcome the support for families.

It is an area of social life about which there are arguments regarding the roles of men and women. Should men go out to work whilst women remain at home to care for the family? What is the impact on the family of women who work? Should men take more responsibility for childrearing and domestic tasks? Feminist thinking holds that childcare and domestic responsibilities are tasks which are undervalued by society and which women are expected to do unpaid. Women are often prevented from taking on higher managerial responsibilities at work, or even from entering the labour market, because of their family responsibilities.

The current government is the first government ever to publish a consultation document on the family. *Supporting Families* brings together a range of government initiatives which aim to support families.

> Family life is the foundation on which our communities, our society and our country are built. ... what all families have a right to expect from government is support. This includes a modern National Health Service equipped to meet their needs; local schools to provide good education for their children; safe streets, strong communities and a welfare system which offers security for those who can't work, and helps those who can into work.
>
> The Rt. Hon. Jack Straw MP,
> Home Secretary,
> Home Office Consultation Paper, 1998

The following initiatives are intended to bring about the vision outlined above, and are taken from the *Supporting Families* consultation paper.

SERVICES AND SUPPORT FOR PARENTS

The government aims to give more support directly to families in the following ways:

- establishing the new National Family and Parenting Institute which is aimed to provide a stronger national focus on family and parenting issues, and helpful guidance, and to improve and develop parenting support by April 1999;
- setting up a free national parenting helpline to give telephone advice to parents and refer them to places where they can gain support locally;
- enhancing the role of health visitors to extend their remit to looking at the whole needs of parents and children, not just their physical health needs. The aim of their new role is to help prevent problems from arising within families in the first place;
- implementing the Sure Start initiative, a new £540-million programme targeting families with multiple difficulties such as poor health, housing or educational achievement or unemployment. The initiative aims to ensure that services work together to benefit families and are offered early so that problems do not become long-term. Every local family will receive a visit from an outreach worker within three months of the baby's birth to assess the needs of the child and give advice to the parents, and support can continue in the home setting if parents do not feel able to access local services. Funding will be made available through local partnerships for a range of services, including:
  - family support
  - childcare
  - primary health care
  - early learning and play
  - training for work
  - help with literacy or numeracy
  - help and advice on parenting problems
  - specific support for parents of children with learning difficulties and emotional and behavioural problems.

  The Sure Start programme will be integrated with government programmes on childcare and education and the New Deal for Communities (see below);

- support for family literacy and mentoring schemes where parents can help their children to learn;
- the introduction of parenthood education into the school curriculum;
- help for grandparents and older people to offer support to families;
- changes in the adoption rules to lift restrictions in some areas.

FINANCIAL SUPPORT FOR FAMILIES

There is widespread concern that children are growing up in poverty. An estimated three million children in the UK are growing up in households where no one works. The current government is making changes in the tax and benefits systems with the aim of giving additional financial help to families. These changes include:

- a Child Benefit increase, by 20 per cent from April 1999, with an additional £2.50 per week for families on Income Support and Family Credit for each child under 11;
- the Working Families Tax Credit (WFTC) which will be introduced from October 1999 to replace Family Credit. The WFTC will contain a childcare tax credit to help with up to 70 per cent of the eligible costs of approved childcare, and provide a guaranteed minimum income, raising the point at which families begin to pay tax;
- the New Deal for Lone Parents on Income Support which provides advice, training and help with finding a job;
- an Education Maintenance Allowance scheme which is being piloted to enable parents with low incomes to support their children in continuing in education after 16;
- a modernisation of the Child Support

Agency in order to simplify and speed up the process so that non-resident fathers are encouraged to contribute to their children's upbringing.

BALANCING HOME AND WORK

There are difficulties for families in trying to balance the demands of work and family life, particularly in terms of childcare and caring for family members who have disabilities, or who are sick or elderly. In the last 10 years, the number of mothers in paid employment has grown from 52 per cent to 62 per cent, whilst the number of mothers with children under 5 has increased from 32 per cent to 51 per cent. Women are expected to form the majority of the anticipated 1.2 million rise in the workforce by 2006. Work is seen as the way in which families can support themselves without needing to rely on the state, but the strain which combining work with family responsibilities can place on family life creates other problems. To combat this, the government has put in place a range of strategies and directives which are aimed to reconcile the balance between work and family life. These include the following.

The National Childcare Strategy

The National Childcare Strategy is an ambitious scheme to double childcare provision to ensure that childcare is available in local communities for children aged 0–14 years through local Early Years Development and Childcare Partnerships. Since the Second World War, the UK government has made it clear that it is the responsibility of the family, not the state, to care for children under statutory school age, with the exception of children who are seen to be in need in some way, so the

National Childcare Strategy is a significant change in social-policy direction. In the UK, childcare has been left to the market to provide, with a range of different providers, mainly in the voluntary and private sector, developing provision to respond to the needs of parents and children in communities. Provision here includes:

- playgroups
- childminding
- after-school clubs
- playschemes
- creches
- full daycare.

The National Childcare Strategy aims to ensure quality childcare which is accessible and affordable to families.

Quality

To ensure quality, the government is taking the following measures:

- establishing Early Excellence Centres across the country to provide models of good practice to demonstrate how the care and education of children can be integrated, and to give support to parents and informal carers;
- improving the regulation of childcare provision;
- establishing out-of-school learning activities;
- developing new standards for early education and childcare;
- developing a new training and qualifications framework for childcare workers, and providing more opportunities for people to enter this field of work.

Affordability

To ensure that childcare is affordable, the government is introducing a new childcare tax credit as part of the Working Families Tax Credit which replaces Family Credit in 1999, and financial support is being given to further-education colleges to help with the costs of childcare for parents undertaking education and training.

Accessibility

The government's aim is to increase childcare places by providing £300 million across England to develop new out-of-school places. All 4-year-olds have access to free education places from September 1998. Information is also seen as a key to ensuring accessibility, and local-authority areas are being asked to develop childcare information services to link with the new national helpline which will set up in 1999.

These aims will be achieved through the Early Years Development and Childcare Partnerships which are established in each local-authority area in England. The partnerships are made up of all the major stakeholders in the childcare sector, including providers from the voluntary, private and public sectors, parents, Training and Enterprise Councils (TECs) and employers, and their purpose is to oversee the development of provision to meet local needs to the required standards.

The National Carer's Strategy

This will look at support for carers, and it is due to be launched shortly.

Family-friendly employee rights

The 1998 White Paper *Fairness at Work* outlined the government's plans to implement both the Part-Time Work Directive by April 2000 to raise the status of the mainly female part-time workforce, and the EU Parental Leave Directive by December 1999. It is proposed to extend maternity rights from 14 to 18 weeks and to reduce the qualifying period for extended maternity leave from 2 years to 1 year. The government has also indicated that it wants to promote sensible working hours (not more than 48 hours per week) and to protect employees who have to take time off to deal with a family crisis, for example, to look after a sick child or parent.

Family-friendly employment practice

The government here wants to promote:

- the business case for family-friendly employment practices in terms of recruitment and retention of staff, and reduced sick leave and absenteeism;
- the economic case for family-friendly employment policies as these increase the number of skilled people in the labour market, enhance financial independence – particularly for women – and improve productivity;
- the social benefits of family-friendly policies as these strengthen families and communities.

STRENGTHENING MARRIAGE

The government is consulting on a range of proposals here, including:

- counselling for couples intending to get married;
- pre-nuptial agreements;
- greater availability of marriage counselling;
- support to parents at critical points such as the birth of a child;
- a reduction of conflict on marriage breakdown through the new divorce process in the Family Law Act 1996 and through changes in the court welfare proceedings.

SUPPORT FOR SERIOUS FAMILY PROBLEMS

The government here particularly wants to tackle:

- *problems with children's learning:* the £500-million Pupil Support Grant aims to cut truancy, unruly behaviour in schools and school exclusions, and to clarify the responsibilities of parents, children and schools through home–school agreements. The target is to cut truancy and exclusions by one-third by 2002. From 1999, all local education authorities are expected to have a parent partnership scheme for parents of children with special educational needs. The government is also considering how the law could be improved to protect children better;
- *youth offences:* the introduction of parenting orders to help parents to change their child's offending behaviour, of child safety orders to enable the courts and the police to intervene at an earlier stage if a child is at risk of offending, of child curfews (ie of measures which prevent children from being on the street between certain times) and of final warnings through the Crime and Disorder Act 1998, aims to protect children at risk of offending and to support parents in dealing with children's offending behaviour;
- *teenage pregnancy:* rates of teenage pregnancy in the UK are higher than anywhere else in the EU, and the government wants to improve education and support services in this area;
- *domestic violence:* there are plans to improve reporting, and for tougher action by the police and courts. Domestic violence is the most common violent crime against women in

England and Wales (according to the 1998 British Crime Survey).

The Ministerial Group on the Family will also be looking at the needs of young men and at support for fathers in its future work. This is as a result of concern about boys' declining educational performance, the loss of traditional 'male' jobs, drugs misuse, teenage fatherhood and the rising suicide rate in young men.

Housing

There are 20.5 million dwellings housing about 50 million people in England (according to the Department of the Environment, Transport and the Regions). Table 8.1 shows who owns or manages these dwellings. Local-authority housing and housing managed by registered social landlords such as *housing associations* are known as *social housing*. This is a very different pattern from that of 80 years ago. People are much more likely to own their own home now, and there is an 80-per-cent reduction in private ·renting. Social housing has grown during this century to a peak of nearly 30 per cent in the 1970s. The Right to Buy scheme which encouraged council tenants to buy their own homes was taken up by 1.3 million council tenants, and accounts for the recent decrease in social housing. There has also been a transfer of many homes from local authorities to housing associations. New houses nowadays tend to be mainly built by the private sector.

Although only 1 per cent of homes in England lack the basic amenities (these are defined as: a kitchen sink, a bath or shower in an inside bathroom, a wash-hand basin with hot and cold water, and an indoor WC), there are still 1.5 million that fail the current housing fitness standard (a nine-point statutory yardstick of health-and-safety-based requirements against which local authorities assess whether dwellings are fit for human habitation). English housing stock is old, and those dwellings that do not pass the fitness standards tend to be older, urban dwellings in the private sector, although problems are also found on some local-authority estates.

There were over 810,000 empty dwellings in April 1997. However, not all of these could be used. For example, about 45 per cent of private-sector empty dwellings lie empty during the selling and buying process. Similar vacancies occur in social housing between lettings, and are

Tenure	Owner-occupied	Local-authority owned and managed	Registered social landlords	Private rented sector
No. of dwellings	13.9 million (68%)	3.6 million (18%)	1 million (5%)	2 million (10%)

Table 8.1 Housing tenure

essential to allow mobility. Some dwellings need renovating to make them fit for occupation, some are in areas where people are not looking for housing, and some may be awaiting demolition.

HOUSING FINANCE

The average price of a house in England in the last quarter of 1997 was £79,000. In the area of social housing, average rents in 1997 were £52.00 per week for new assured tenancies let by housing associations and £41.00 per week for local-authority tenancies. In the private rented sector, rents averaged £76.00 a week in 1996/97.

Local authorities are currently only allowed to spend 25 per cent of their receipts from sales of council housing, in order to limit public expenditure. The rest of the money is encouraged to be used to repay debts.

Central and local government financial support in terms of public spending and tax reliefs is about £18 billion each year, or nearly £1,000 per dwelling on average. (See Table 8.2.) Private investors have put a total of nearly £12 billion into social housing since 1988.

THE ROLE OF LOCAL AUTHORITIES IN HOUSING

Local authorities are responsible for making sure that the best use is made of all housing in their areas. They are expected to assess local needs and produce comprehensive housing strategies, in partnership with tenants, residents and other members of the local community. Since the 1988 Housing Act, housing associations have moved from complementing the work of local authorities to becoming the main providers of new social housing. While local authorities' responsibilities for providing and managing social housing have reduced, the importance of their role as strategic enablers has grown. Increasingly, local authorities are taking a more corporate approach, linking the services they provide to maximise their effectiveness.

Local authorities are responsible for allocating tenancies in their own housing stock and in a large proportion of housing-association homes to which they have nomination rights. The law requires authorities to allocate tenancies only to people included on a housing register (or waiting list) and in accordance with a published allocation scheme. Some people are excluded from the register by law

Old English housing stock

Source of financial support	Type/area of expenditure	1997/98
Capital allocations to local authorities	• Renovation of housing stock; • Grants to Registered Social Landlords to build new social housing; • Cash incentives to help social housing tenants become home owners in the private sector; • Grants to renovate private-sector homes; • Grants to carry out adaptations to homes for disabled people.	£754 million.
Regeneration programmes	• Housing Action Trusts • Estate Action • City Challenge • Single Regeneration Budget.	£1.3 billion.
Housing Benefit	To help tenants with low incomes (4 million households) pay rent.	£10 billion (including rent rebates).
Tax relief	Mortgage interest payments (MIRAS), to reduce the cost of buying a home.	£1.4 billion.
Income Support	Mortgage interest payments to help people retain their homes when they have lost their income.	£900 million.
Discounts	To help tenants in social housing buy the homes they rent.	£900 million.
Estates Renewal Challenge Fund	A fund for the improvement of poorer-quality council estates.	£100 million.
Local-authority housing revenue accounts	Subsidy to support revenue expenditure	£640 million.
Local-authority capital receipts and revenue contributions to capital outlay	Capital building and improvement works.	£1.1 billion.
Housing corporation	Funding for Registered Social Landlords to develop social housing.	£673 million.

Table 8.2 Government housing finance

(people subject to immigration control, for example); outside of these groups, it is open to authorities to decide who does or does not qualify. The allocation scheme must give priority to certain specified households: those in unsatisfactory, insecure or temporary accommodation; a group that includes dependent children, pregnant women or people who need housing on medical or welfare grounds; low-income or non-working households; and homeless people with a priority need for accommodation.

HOMELESSNESS

By law, local housing authorities must assist those people who apply to them for help because they are actually homeless or are about to become homeless. Where people applying for assistance have become homeless through no fault of their own and fall within a 'priority need' group, the authority must either help them to obtain suitable accommodation from a private landlord in the area or, if this is not available, secure suitable accommodation for them. In either case, accommodation must be available for at least two years. The priority-need group includes families with dependent children, pregnant women, people who are vulnerable in some way (for example, through old age, disability or mental illness) and those made homeless by an emergency (such as flood or fire). During 1997, local authorities in England accepted 103,340 households as unintentionally homeless and in priority need. Everyone accepted as unintentionally homeless and in priority need has the right to go on the local authority's housing register and be considered for a permanent tenancy in social housing. Shelter, the homelessness charity, estimates that there are a total of 400,000 homeless people in England alone. In 1998, 26 per cent of those people accepted as homeless lost their last home because friends or relatives could no longer accommodate them, 24 per cent did so because of relationship breakdown, and 6 per cent did so because of mortgage arrears.

The 1996–97 Survey of English Housing shows the following trends:

- Fewer young people are occupying housing because of a fall in the birth rate and a growing tendency for young adults to live with their parents. Those who leave home tend to rent privately.
- There was a rise of 330,000 in the number of lone parents who had never been married between 1984 and 1996–97, corresponding with a significant increase in private-sector renting. The proportion renting privately rose from 5 per cent to 15 per cent, whilst the proportion in social-sector housing (ie council housing and housing associations) fell from 85 per cent to 73 per cent. There was a smaller increase in lone parents who had previously been married: up by 190,000. Most of the additional numbers (120,000) were owner-occupiers. Proportions renting privately also increased, whilst the proportion renting from a council or housing association fell from 54 per cent to 44 per cent.
- More cohabiting couples than married couples rent their homes. Cohabiting couples with children are far more likely than married couples of the same age to be renting from a social landlord: 49 per cent compared with 25 per cent below age 30. There are correspondingly fewer who are owner-occupiers: 34 per cent compared with 62 per cent for those below 30; but there is not a great difference here in the proportions

renting privately. Cohabiting couples without children, by contrast, are more likely than their married counterparts to be renting privately, particularly in the group aged under 30 where 32 per cent rent privately, as compared with 14 per cent of married couples. Below age 45, 60 per cent are owners, compared with 80 per cent of married couples. The proportions renting from a social landlord are low.

- Despite the decrease in the total number of council tenants, the number of people moving has shown little change since 1984. The percentage who had moved in the previous 12 months rose from 9 per cent in 1988 to 12 per cent in 1996/97. However, between 1984 and 1996/97, there were large increases in the numbers of housing-association and private tenants who had moved: the number of housing-association tenants moving rose from 50,000 to 70,000 (15

per cent to 18 per cent), and the number of private renters moving rose from 450,000 to 830,000 (24 per cent to 40 per cent).

The current government has the following aims for housing:

- to integrate housing and regeneration, using schemes like the New Deal for Communities to renovate existing housing stock;
- to link the structure of social-sector renting to Housing Benefit reform;
- to ensure better tenant participation in housing matters;
- to separate local-authority housing management responsibilities from the local authorities' strategic role in planning for housing with the private sector and registered social landlords;
- to create a Housing Inspectorate under the Audit Commission to ensure Best Value.

Health and social services

Although people now live longer and are in better health, there is a concern that health inequalities are becoming greater as poorer people are ill more often and die sooner. There is also a concern that services are organised more to meet the needs of the institutions which provide them than to meet the needs of the people who use them. In particular, the government believes that the care-in-the-community policy has failed people with mental-health problems, with the result that these people have not been given adequate support and have been a danger to themselves and others. It also believes that

the current system has failed children in the care system (Children Looked After), as the statistics show that these young people are much more likely to underachieve. In order to address the issues outlined above, the government is implementing a range of policies to modernise health and social services over a 10-year period.

One of the fundamental principles which underpins these new policies is that of partnership, allowing the complex needs of people to be more effectively met. The new Primary Care Groups (PCGs) are run by boards which include

GPs, nurses, a social-services officer, a representative of the health authority and a local member of the public. These boards take responsibility for the planning and funding of health services for the community they serve – usually a population of about 100,000. They must plan to:

- improve the health of the local population
- improve local primary and community services
- commission hospital services for local patients.

The government hopes that the PCGs will end the internal market in the NHS and help modernise health services. Health Action Zones targeting particular areas of need, and Health Improvement Programmes which are local vehicles for meeting national health priorities, will also promote partnership working.

Value for money is also a key element in current government policies, with new targets for asset sales, a campaign against fraud and a drive for efficiency. The government aims to set targets for achievement against which further funding will be allocated.

Responsiveness of services is another area for modernisation. There is a drive to reduce waiting lists and waiting times, and the introduction of NHS Direct, the telephone advice helpline, aims to give people advice on how to look after themselves, as well as directing them to appropriate health services in the NHS. In addition, there is an increased emphasis on ensuring that users' views help shape services. Information technology is expected to support the achievement of these aims.

In social services, there is a new emphasis on rehabilitation and on reducing dependence where possible, and changes in the regulation of services to better protect vulnerable users.

The national priorities for modernisation, together with the agencies responsible for them, are shown in Table 8.3.

Children's welfare

Many children are in need, according to the Children Act 1989, and about 55,000 are looked after by local authorities. The needs of these children in terms of their risk of neglect or significant harm, their poor life chances and poor health have been highlighted by the 1997 Utting Report *Children's Safeguards Review*. The concerns are particularly about the poor educational achievement of children looked after by local authorities, the large number of unsuccessful placements for individual children (often due to inadequate assessments in the first place), and

the lack of support for young people leaving the care system. There is also concern about the number of children who are removed from the child-protection register but who have to be put back on later. The new Quality Protects programme is designed to improve this. Both Health and Social Services will be involved in the multi-agency youth offending teams which are being set up by local authorities in conjunction with education and health authorities and the police and probation services under the Crime and Disorder Act.

Social Services	Shared	NHS
• Children's welfare	• Cutting health inequalities	• Waiting lists/waiting times
• Inter-agency working	• Mental health	• Primary care
• Regulation	• Promoting independence	• Coronary heart disease
		• Cancer

Source: Department of Health (1998) *Modernising Health and Social Services.*

Table 8.3 Current (1998) Labour-government national modernisation priorities, and the agencies responsible

Mental health

A new national service framework for mental health is due to be published by April 1999 to ensure that there is a reduction in the rate of suicide and undetermined injury in people with mental-health problems. There will be 24-hour staffed accommodation and a 24-hour helpline, access to early intervention services, and day and residential care services. It is hoped that partnerships working in this area will improve services.

Education and training

There is currently a significant emphasis on education and training for all ages. This chapter has already mentioned some of the initiatives currently under way to improve the quality of and access to education and training for the whole population. Table 8.4 outlines some of the principal policies currently being enacted in this area.

REGULATION

The Qualification and Curriculum Authority (QCA) is the statutory body which advises the government on the curriculum, school examinations and assessment, and is responsible for the regulation of *vocational qualifications*. There are similar organisations in Scotland (the Scottish Qualifications Authority (SQA) and in Wales (the Qualification, Curriculum and Assessment Authority (ACCAC)).

The newly established National Training Organisations (NTOs) are employer-led sector organisations which establish and review the National Occupational Standards for their sector (against which the National Vocational Qualifications are then assessed).

Together with the QCA, the NTOs will establish qualification and training frameworks for each sector which clarify the qualifications needed for specific occupations and career-progression routes. This work is expected to be complete by 2001.

The environment

There is a growing awareness of environmental issues and of the need for policies to ensure **sustainability**. The 1992 Earth Summit in Rio de Janeiro was an important catalyst for environmental policy. In particular, it was recognised that local action is necessary to tackle what are often seen as global problems. Local Agenda 21 listed the environmental actions which needed to be taken to integrate economic and environmental policies in order to have an integrated approach to sustainability. In the UK, much responsibility lies at the local level, with the target that all local authorities should put in place Agenda 21 strategies by the year 2000. This represents a change in national policy which is now more firmly backing local economic policy initiatives to link environmental improvement to local economic change. National policies are aiming to act as a bridge between European policies and local action concerned with economic and social sustainability.

Sustainable Development: the UK Strategy (Department of the Environment, 1994) was the first structured approach to integrating social and economic as well as environmental goals as outlined in Agenda 21 and other international agreements reached at the Earth Summit in 1992. This policy statement was intended to provide a framework for sustainable development for the UK for the next 20 years across different sectors of the economy and all sections of society.

The government has published *Opportunities for Change*, a consultation paper on a revised strategy (Department of the Environment, Transport and the Regions, 1998). The new vision of sustainable development is based on four broad objectives (adapted from these DETR documents):

1 *Social progress which recognises the needs of everyone.* This objective recognises that it is not enough to focus on economic and environmental policies if whole groups in society, or parts of the country, are excluded. It aims to reduce the health risks caused by poverty, poor housing, unemployment and pollution, and to ensure that meeting local needs does not involve treating others elsewhere in the world unfairly;

2 *Effective protection of the environment.* This objective aims to act to limit global environmental threats such as climate change, to protect human health and safety from hazards such as poor air quality and toxic chemicals, and to safeguard wildlife, landscapes and historic buildings;

3 *Prudent use of natural resources.* This objective aims to ensure that non-renewable resources like oil and gas are used efficiently, that alternatives are developed to replace them and that renewable resources, such as water, are used in ways that do not endanger these latter resources or cause serious damage or pollution;

Initiative	Target group	Detail
Early Years Development	3-, 4- and 5-year-olds.	Each local authority in England and Wales now has an Early Years Development Plan to ensure access to free education places for all 4-year-olds, and to set targets for the expansion of places for 3-year-olds. The Desirable Learning Outcomes guide the framework for provision for the education of 4-year-olds. These are currently under review.
Assessment	5–16-year-olds.	In England, Wales and Northern Ireland, there is a baseline assessment of all pupils when they start school. This is followed by regular assessment by the Standard Assessment Tests (SATs).
National Curriculum	5–16-year-olds.	All state schools in England, Wales and Northern Ireland conform to the national curricula. In Scotland, there is no prescribed curriculum but instead guidelines which provide the curriculum framework. From September 1998, the primary curriculum in England and Wales has been modified to concentrate on teaching literacy and numeracy through the prescribed literacy and numeracy hours.
Learning Support	Schoolchildren when out of school.	Funding is being made available to provide homework support for children.
Excellence for All: Meeting Special Educational Needs: a programme of action	All children with special educational needs (SEN).	The action plan here aims to set high expectations for children with SEN, support parents, increase the number of children in mainstream schools, and provide more professional development for teachers. A simplified Code of Practice for children with SEN will be introduced in 2000/2001.
Home–School Agreements	All children, in order to reduce truancy and school exclusions.	All schools are required to have written home–school contracts drawn up in consultation with parents. The aim is to involve parents in raising the educational achievements of their children and to help combat unacceptable behaviour.
Education Action Zones	Areas with particular problems.	Building on local partnerships between clusters of schools, local education authorities (LEAs), parents, businesses and Training and Enterprise Councils (TECs), the aim of Education Action Zones is to improve literacy and numeracy levels.

Lifelong Learning

Adults.

The government is implementing a range of initiatives to encourage adult access to training and education to ensure an adaptable workforce. These include:

- open and distance learning;
- flexible modes of study;
- The University for Industry which uses a multi-media learning network to bring learning opportunities to the home, the workplace and the community;
- Learning direct: a national telephone helpline offering advice on training and learning support;
- Individual Learning Accounts;
- The Basic Skills Agency which aims to improve literacy and numeracy levels for all ages.

Table 8.4 Principal current (1998) Labour-government policies to improve the quality of, and access to, education and training

Targets for 11-year-olds	Targets for 16-year-olds	Targets for young people	Targets for adults	Targets for organisations
Level 4 or above in national tests in English and Mathematics.	50% with 5 higher-grade GCSEs.	85% of 19-year-olds with a level-2 qualification (ie 5 GCSEs at grade A–C; NVQ level 2; intermediate GNVQ).	50% with a level-3 qualification (2 A levels; NVQ level 3; Advanced GNVQ).	45% of medium-sized or large organisations recognised as Investors in People.
	95% with at least 1 GCSE.	60% of 21-year-olds with a level-3 qualification (2 A levels; NVQ level 3; Advanced GNVQ).	28% with a level-4 qualification (NVQ level 4; a degree; a higher-level vocational qualification).	10,000 small organisations recognised as Investors in People.
			A learning participation target for adults is due to be announced.	

Table 8.5   The national learning targets for England for 2002

4 *The maintenance of high and stable levels of economic growth and employment.* This objective aims to ensure that everyone in Britain has a share in high living standards and greater job opportunities.

UK environmental policy recognises the need for a competitive economy and emphasises co-ordination across policy areas such as economy, education, health or employment. *Opportunities for Change* identifies regeneration projects as supporting 'communities for people', reinforcing the messages about capacity building, about partnership, about the need to counter social exclusion, and about the importance of sustainable principles in both urban and rural communities. The government also accepts the importance of building the principles of sustainability into its strategic planning, and the new Regional Development Agencies (RDAs) will have a specific objective of promoting sustainable economic development and social and physical regeneration, and of co-ordinating the work of regional and local partners in areas such as training, investment, regeneration and business support. The RDAs will be established by statute as government-sponsored public bodies, with boards which are business-led and which reflect the perspectives and needs of each region, and the main interest here is in greater regional coherence and the effective delivery of government programmes. They will have significant budgets of their own, and will contribute their regional perspective to the work of other central, regional and local programmes and bodies. They will cover the different government office regions, and will aim to:

- enhance the employment prospects, education and skills of local people;
- address social exclusion, and enhance opportunities for the disadvantaged through community development;
- promote sustainable regeneration, improving and protecting the environment and infrastructure;
- improve both the quality of life of local people and their capacity to participate in regeneration activities;
- encourage more effective integration of programmes through partnerships and the involvement of local communities and voluntary groups;
- support and promote growth in local economies and businesses.

Local government reform

The current government believes that local authorities should be more in touch with people and provide the vision for local communities, and aims to introduce a new framework which will provide opportunities and incentives for councils to modernise so that they:

- are in touch with local people
- have strong and effective links with business
- have modern management structures
- deliver best value.

New models of political management for

councils are being considered. Each model separates the executive role from the back-bench role and clarifies the roles of the councillors. These models include:

- *a directly elected executive mayor with a cabinet.* The mayor will be elected by local people and will appoint a cabinet from among the councillors;
- *a cabinet with a leader.* The leader will be elected by the council, and the cabinet will be made up of councillors either appointed by the leader or elected by the council;
- *a directly elected mayor with a council manager.* The mayor will be elected by local people, with a full-time manager appointed by the council.

There are plans to improve local democracy by holding more frequent local elections and making it easier to vote. Councils will be required to adopt a **code of conduct**, based on a national model, which councillors will be under a duty to observe. There will also be a new code of conduct for council employees, built into their conditions of employment.

Councils will have a duty to secure best value in the provision of services. The current Compulsory Competitive Tendering (CCT) regime is being abolished in favour of best value.

New national performance indicators for efficiency, cost and quality will be set, and councils will set and publish their own local targets against these indicators. Councils will be required to undertake performance reviews of all their services over a five-year period, starting with those that are performing the worst. The reviews will:

- look at why and how a service is being provided;
- compare the performance of the services;
- consult with local taxpayers, service users and the wider business community on how services can be improved;
- ensure fair competition for service provision.

There will be new audit and inspection arrangements, including a new Best Value Inspectorate, working with other Inspectorates, which will oversee an objective and independent process of regular inspection of all local services.

Local government reform aims to ensure that councils promote the economic, social and environmental well-being of their area and work with other public, private and voluntary organisations and with local people to do this. Their powers to work in partnership to tackle cross-cutting issues and promote social inclusion will be strengthened.

There will be a single capital finance 'pot' which is aimed to help councils to use resources more flexibly and plan for the long term. Councils will no longer have to set aside, for debt repayment, receipts from the sales of assets (other than council houses).

Devolution

The present government was elected with a **mandate** to modernise the way in which Britain is run. **Devolution** of power from Westminster – to Scotland, Wales and the English regions – is hoped to play an important part in that process, with the aim of giving real responsibility over local affairs to those living in the nation or region concerned. The devolution process aims to strengthen rather than undermine the unity of the UK as a whole.

Scotland has not had its own Parliament for almost 300 years. But a **referendum** in Scotland in September 1997 voted in favour of the creation of a Scottish Parliament. The first elections are due in 1999, and the Parliament should be in place by 2000.

In Wales, a similar referendum gained a narrower vote for a Welsh Assembly.

The development of the Regional Development Agencies in government office areas in England can also be seen as part of the move towards devolution.

Key themes

This brief look at current and emerging social policy has some clear common themes which underpin the approach of the current government.

USER PARTICIPATION

In all policies, the views of users are becoming more important, whether in health and social services or in housing. Those who are implementing policies are being asked to undertake more research into the views of users and to consult more to ensure that policy is meeting needs. Users are now being involved in decision-making.

MONITORING EFFECTIVENESS

There is an increasing emphasis on the monitoring and measuring of effectiveness and efficiency. New inspectorates are being established, and regulatory systems are being reviewed. There is a clear intention to link value for money with quality at all times, and to ensure the effective collection of data by which to monitor services.

PARTNERSHIP

Organisations and services which have worked in isolation are now being asked to work together to find effective solutions to social problems. This is challenging for all concerned, and is involving time and effort to rethink habitual ways of working.

There will inevitably be an impact on service delivery here as patterns of services change so as to be delivered by different partners. The private and voluntary sectors are expected to be significant providers in future personal and social services. Will Social Services become a purchaser rather than a provider of services in the future?

Future social policy

The policies outlined in this chapter are either newly implemented, projected or at the consultation stage. Social policies will change, and new policies are being drafted on a daily basis. To keep abreast of current developments, there are a range of resources available:

- newspapers
- broadcast media
- statistical publications, such as *Social Trends*, which can be found in local libraries
- research publications by organisations such as the Policy Studies Institute
- the Internet, and in particular the UK open government website which gives details of all the latest press releases, and from which policy documents can often be downloaded. The website address is www.open.gov.uk.

CHAPTER 9

MAKING POLICY A REALITY

This chapter will enable the reader to relate policy to practice. It is divided into a number of scenarios, each of which focuses on a different social issue. These scenarios detail real life problems/issues/difficulties that social policies are designed to tackle. It allows the reader to consider the policy implications in each case, draw on the strategies currently being used to deal with the issues presented in the scenario and consider for themselves possible alternatives. The final exercise is written as an assignment, and focuses on funding.

How to use this chapter

There is no one way of using the scenarios in this chapter. They are designed to provoke thought and discussion. You can work on them alone, in pairs, in small groups or in a large group. They can form the basis of an assignment, a research project or a personal or class-based exercise. There are no right or wrong answers. It is for you to develop your own hypothesis and consider the results in the light of your own research/debate.

By way of an introduction to the different scenarios, you will find a number of general questions. You can apply these to any of the scenarios, and they will point you in the direction of relevant policies and the strategies designed to implement these. (Chapter 8 has provided details of the policies and initiatives you should consider.) In addition, a specific activity is included for each scenario. This activity will presuppose that you have considered some of the general questions involved.

SOME REMINDERS

- A social policy is any policy that regulates either the organisation and the delivery of services or resource allocation in the society in which it has been developed.
- A social policy is usually broadly based and may have a number of objectives.
- A variety of initiatives or strategies may be used to implement policy.

Into the new millennium, the following

areas of social policy underpin the delivery of services and resource allocation:

- strengthening the family and marriage
- social inclusion
- law and order
- social and economic regeneration
- employment
- partnership, participation and 'joined-up thinking'.

The scenarios presented will be based on these themes.

General questions

1 Identify the client group or groups involved.
2 Identify the primary (ie most important) issue for social policy outlined in the scenario.
3 Identify any secondary (ie important but not the main concern) issues for social policy outlined in the scenario.
4 Which social policy is being addressed in the scenario?
5 What current strategies or policy initiatives are being used to deal with the issue(s) presented in the scenario, nationally/regionally/locally?
6 Which agency or agencies are responsible for ensuring that current strategies or initiatives are being implemented?
7 Compare the strategies/initiatives employed in England, Scotland, Wales or Northern Ireland

- with each other, or
- with a member of the European Union, eg France, Spain, Italy or Portugal, or
- with a non-EEC member, eg America, Australia, Kenya or China.

8 What, if any, legislation regulates the issues, situation or policy presented?
9 What, if any, European Directive regulates the issue, situation or policy presented?
10 What are the implications for agencies working together (ie in partnership) and attempting to devise joint strategies (ie 'joined-up thinking')?

Please note: the characters in the scenarios are fictitious and are not based on any persons known to the authors either in part or in total.

Scenario 1: a community in need

Nonesuch Estate is on the edge of a large city. The majority of the housing is in poor condition. Some is privately owned, but most is rented from the local authority or housing trust. A small amount is privately rented. The housing stock consists mainly of low-rise flats and houses, but two high-rise blocks dominate the skyline. The estate was built in the early 1960s. The estate has a population of 3,000. The majority of people living on the estate have moved there from other areas of the town, and for most it was not a positive choice. Both the housing trust and the local authority tend to move hard-to-place tenants there. Few green spaces exist on the estate, and the play equipment available is old and in need of repair. The local council is loath to do this work. It maintains that vandalism on the estate makes it a waste of money. As a consequence, there are no safe places for the youngest children to play. Public transport is costly and mainly runs at peak times only. Only one-third of households own a car.

The average age of tenants in the high-rise blocks is 25 years old. At least a third of the children living on the estate are being raised in lone-parent households. The estate has a higher-than-average number of teenage parents. The population is 87 per cent White European, with 10 per cent of Asian origin (including Chinese) and 3 per cent Afro-Caribbean. 60 per cent of the potential working population on the estate is unemployed.

The local school's Standard Attainment Test (SATs) results indicate that the children are failing to achieve the appropriate standard for their age in numeracy and literacy tasks. A recent OFSTED inspection acknowledged the sterling work of the school, and highlighted social deprivation as one reason for poor results, another being a high staff turnover.

Local Health Visitors have attempted to engage parents in health-education classes, but a lack of resources has placed limits on what they were able to achieve. They suggest that many young children are eating an unbalanced diet due to low incomes and a lack of knowledge about meal planning. Whilst the children are outwardly healthy, they have concerns about the long-term effects of poor diet on the children.

The police keep a relatively low profile but are aware that drug pushing and taking is endemic on the estate. Most young men under 25 years are unemployed, and there is little for them to do with their time. Drugs are cheaper and more easily available to the under-18-year-olds than alcohol. Some resort to crime to feed their drug habit. Gang fights and joyriding appear to be the weekend pastime for some of the estate's young people. The police are concerned that the age of drug taking and involvement in petty crime is getting younger. The youth club was recently closed down because of gang fights.

SPECIFIC ACTIVITIES

You are the project leader for the Community in Need Initiative (CINI). CINI is a non-profit-making, lottery-funded project. You have £50,000 to spend on community initiatives.

Along with a small group of community-development workers, it is your task to:

1 Map the issues that are disadvantaging this community. Your analysis should include:

- what
- why
- who
- the potential impact
- a list of priorities.

2 Engage the local community and encourage it to develop ideas.

- How do you intend to do this?
- Where?
- And at what cost?
- What help might you need, and from whom?
- What difficulties might there be?

3 Present at least three possible initiatives aimed at dealing with the issues you prioritised earlier. Your presentation should include:

- the idea
- the aims and objectives
- who will benefit
- costing
- why it should be chosen
- how it will be achieved
- the level of community involvement.

4 Discuss and vote on the initiatives, or list your initiatives in order of merit if you are working alone.

Local authority housing

Scenario 2: Rory

Rory is 18 years old and has been living rough in London for two years. Rory occasionally stays in a night shelter but mostly lives in a cardboard box under a railway bridge. He only sleeps in doorways as a last resort and generally when he has been moved on by the police.

Rory makes his living by begging and running errands for what he calls 'dodgy characters'. He eats one meal a day, usually in a small café in Hammersmith. The proprietor knows him and sometimes lets him take a shower.

Rory is 'clean': he does not take drugs or drink alcohol. However, when he is really short of cash, he has engaged in sex for payment – turned tricks for 'gentlemen', as he calls them. Aside from eating, his money is spent on slot machines: he got hooked when he was 11 years old and is now firmly addicted. His other major expense is street protection. He has to pay to sleep under the bridge; if not, he gets beaten up.

Rory's life on the streets began when he left care. He spent all of his teenage years living in a residential unit for boys who were deemed 'beyond parental control'. Rory has never known his birth father. He has not seen his mother since he went into care at the age of 10. He has no birth siblings. He has two stepsisters aged four and six years, but they have never met him. Rory used to see his granddad, but he thinks he must be dead by now.

Rory was a bright boy. His teachers believed him capable of A levels, and were very disappointed when he left school. He has eight GCSEs, all grade A–C. Rory says he had to leave school because his care order expired and he had to leave the chil-

dren's home. He was offered supported accommodation by his social worker but decided to go to London and get a job. On his first night, he was robbed of all his money and possessions. He says he tried to phone his social worker but she had left, and a duty officer told him his case was closed. Since then, Rory has made do! He believes that all he needs is a leg up and some help to quit his gambling habit, which he says got worse because he was forced to live on the streets. He says it's an escape; it keeps him sane.

SPECIFIC ACTIVITIES

A night-shelter worker gets a call from the police asking the shelter to accommodate

A homeless young person

a young man one night. Rory has been beaten and his cardboard home destroyed. A medical at the police station has passed him fit to leave. The police found him in a daze beside his burning cardboard home. Rory is provided with a bed. As he looks unwell, the next day the staff call in the doctor. Rory is prescribed bed rest for bruised ribs. It is not the shelter's policy to accommodate people during the day other than in a medical exception, and such an exception is made here. This gives the staff time to get to know him and listen to his story. In the afternoon, he helps with some book work.

At a team meeting that night, it is agreed to pass Rory on to a sister organisation specialising in rehabilitation and home finding. Rory agrees to this. You are assigned as Rory's rehabilitation buddy.

What next for Rory . . . ?

1 How best do you approach Rory?
2 What are the priorities for Rory?
3 How might he be helped to achieve his priorities?
4 What will help him succeed?
5 What might push him to return to the streets?
6 What lessons can we learn from Rory's story for other children in care?
7 What local, regional or national strategies are currently in place that could benefit Rory?

Scenario 3: Hilda and Emily

Hilda and Emily live in a small market town. They have lived in the same town all their lives. Hilda was born in, and owns, the house in which they reside. Hilda is 80 years old. She recently fell and broke her hip. She was hospitalised, and is currently staying in a convalescent unit a couple of streets from her home. Emily visits her every day. Her most recent fall has left Hilda quite frail, and she finds it difficult to move around. To complicate matters, she has acute arthritis and has great difficulty using her hands; tasks such as dressing, washing and cooking are virtually impossible for her. Emily is 82 years old. She is hard of hearing but in general good health.

The convalescent home is pushing for a decision to be made about Hilda's future. An assessment undertaken by a social worker asserts:

- that Hilda could not return home and be cared for by Emily as neither of the women is fit enough to care for the other;
- that the house is very large and difficult to maintain, with many of the rooms shut up and the age and design of the house making it difficult to adapt;
- that the only income the two receive is a state pension;
- that the only asset they have is the house;
- that the two women have no family to assist in their support in or out of the home;
- that the two women have been surviving on one, often cold, meal a day, only heating their sitting room for three hours a day;
- that the women receive no visitors to the house and have no telephone for emergencies;

- that Hilda and Emily enjoy a lesbian relationship that has never been openly acknowledged by the women in the local community, which they wish to remain the case;
- that Hilda and Emily are fearful of separation and of people knowing their personal business.

The social worker recommends:

- that the house be sold to assist in the payment of private residential care;
- that Hilda and Emily be able to share a room in their new home.

The search for a placement proves very difficult. Finding a residential home locally that can accommodate two women in the same room appears impossible. The three homes in the local town all have a policy of putting married couples into shared rooms, whilst single people get a room of their own. Only one currently has a double room vacant. They do not want to give this room to Hilda and Emily because single rooms are available. They do not want to, as they see it, 'block' a double room. One of the other homes is full, and the third has two single rooms available. Hilda and Emily have visited all three homes and prefer the one with a double room. They are adamant that they will not leave home unless they can be roomed together. Hilda discharged herself from the convalescent unit, and Emily is now struggling to care for her. The social worker is concerned for their joint welfare.

The social worker has made inquiries and found a residential care home for older lesbians about 10 miles away. This home would be more than pleased to accommodate Hilda and Emily. This unit is designed around small bungalows that have their own bedroom, bathroom and sitting room. The fees are subsidised by a charity for older lesbians in cases where the full cost cannot be met.

SPECIFIC ACTIVITIES

As the social worker, you have a problem: you have tried to get the residential home with the double room to see reason, but you cannot sway its opinion. You feel you might stand more of a chance if you could reveal the sexuality of the two women. However, you have no idea how the staff might react since, to your knowledge, this issue has not been raised before. You personally liked the out-of-town residential home, but cannot be sure how Hilda and Emily would react.

1 List the possible advantages and disadvantages, social, emotional and physical, of Hilda and Emily:
   - being forced by circumstances to take single rooms;
   - being forced by circumstances to 'come out' and declare their lesbian relationship so that they can share a room;
   - being forced by circumstances to leave the town they have lived in all their lives.
2 Research other possible alternatives.
3 What prejudice might Hilda and Emily face if their sexuality became known to the staff and residents of the local care homes?
4 Write an organisational policy that specifically deals with the issue of sexuality in the allocation of vacancies and the treatment of clients in residential settings.
5 Would you consider a social policy that strengthens the family and marriage as supportive or a disadvantage for those who are not heterosexual?
6 Is there any policy that supports people like Hilda and Emily?

Scenario 4: the Lincoln Family

The Lincoln family consists of:

- Vanessa, aged 25
- Brian, aged 35
- Daniel, aged 16
- Josie, aged 7
- Philip, aged 5
- Sian, aged 4
- Carl, aged 3.

The family lives in a three-bedroom high-rise flat on Nonesuch Estate. They have been waiting for a move to a bigger home for two years. Currently, Daniel, Philip and Carl share a room. This is causing a lot of problems. Daniel is from Brian's first marriage. He has lived with them for a year. He comes in late at night and wakes up the younger boys. Vanessa is sure he smokes dope in the room, and she is worried it is having an effect on the others: they are hard to wake in the morning and seem lethargic for their age. One morning, she found a girl in the room, and they had a terrible row, resulting in Daniel hitting Vanessa. Daniel is unemployed.

Brian has been unemployed for three years. He has a temper that he finds hard to control and has been known to beat up both Vanessa and Daniel. He has recently been offered a job at a new sports complex opening in a month's time. He is really excited about this opportunity.

Vanessa is currently taking tranquillisers to calm her nerves. She has a part-time job at a local supermarket. Once Brian starts work, she fears she will have to give up work because of childcare. As work is her only means of stress relief, she is very upset. Also, the extra cash would help them clear their debts and get on their feet.

Josie is Vanessa's daughter from a previous relationship. Josie's father lives locally and sees her occasionally. He is supposed to support her but is not regular in his payments. Josie is confident and outgoing. However, her teachers are concerned about her progress in school. She seems to struggle with reading and writing, although her maths work is above average. The teachers notice that Josie copes much better if she can tape her answers to questions.

Philip has recently started school. He is happy to attend and gets on well with his peers. Like Vanessa, his teacher is concerned that he is lethargic, taking a good few hours in the morning to wake up properly.

Both Sian and Carl attend a local playgroup two mornings a week. Sian has been offered a place in the local school nursery starting next term. The playgroup is also extending its hours, and Sian could stay and attend for five mornings a week. Vanessa likes the playgroup, and so does Sian. Vanessa is unsure what to do. The school is pressuring her to place Sian in the nursery. Sian says she wants to stay with her friends at the playgroup.

SPECIFIC ACTIVITIES

Take each family member in turn and complete the following grid (an example is given for you):

Name	Issue	Comment	Policy strategy
Sian	Playgroup vs Nursery.	The school cannot force Vanessa to send Sian to the school nursery, and has no right to deny her a place if she stays in the playgroup.	National Childcare Strategy

Once you have identified the issues and commented on them, complete the second grid which follows below (an example is given for you).

Name	Possible solution	Action	By whom
Sian	Leave Sian in the playgroup.	Refuse a place in the school nursery and enrol Sian for five mornings at the playgroup.	Vanessa, in consultation with the playgroup.

Scenario 5: Jessica

Jessica is 32 years old and recently widowed. She has three children: Lawrence, aged 9 years, and Raymond, aged 12 years, who both attend local schools. Her youngest child, May, is 4 years old and attends the local school nursery five mornings a week. The family are of Nigerian origin. Most of their extended family live in Nigeria or some 50 miles distant.

Jessica and her husband had not considered his early death, and as such had taken out no insurance or pension policy to help offset his income. Jessica is determined that she is not going to lose her home, and is very willing to work. She realises that in the long term what she needs is not a job but a career, which will involve her in retraining.

Jessica has not worked for 12 years, preferring to stay at home and care for her children. She left school with 9 GCSEs grades B–D. She went to work for an accountancy firm, and is a self-taught touch typist. She has done bookwork and filing, and for the last six months of her employment, she acted as Administrative Supervisor. In this role, she was additionally responsible for answering customer queries, allocating work to a team of six admin assistants and taking minutes. She has never used a computer, however, and is unfamiliar with current office practice. In the short term, Jessica would like to work in a similar environment. In the long term, she wants to train as an accountant.

During the last 12 years, Jessica has been treasurer for the local playgroup, the local Women's Health Centre and her gardening club. She also edits the Women's Health Club newsletter.

SPECIFIC ACTIVITIES

1 Write or telephone a few accountancy firms. Ask if you could have a copy of a job description and person specification for a Scale 1 admin person. If they are unhappy about supplying these documents, ask if you could interview someone to find out what skills and qualifications they would require of a new entrant.

2 Once you have some idea of the job requirements and skills needed to become a Scale 1 admin assistant in an accountants office, identify Jessica's skill deficits.

3 Explore ways in which Jessica could acquire these skills and what help is available to support her in retraining and in finding work.

4 Create a career map for Jessica that reflects her short-term needs but results in her achieving her long-term aim.

5 Write up Jessica's CV.

6 Research some pension and insurance schemes. Would any of those you looked at provide Jessica and her children with more security, if she and her husband had had such policies?

7 What prejudice might affect Jessica's search for work?

8 Once Jessica finds a job, she will need to consider childcare. What are her alternatives here? List the advantages and disadvantages of each, including cost. Your answer to this question should be based on what would be available to Jessica if she lived on your street and her children went to the local school.

Scenario 6: Maria

Maria is 20 years old. She is from Croatia. She arrived in Britain with no immigrant visa. She lives in a bedsit with another Croatian woman in a similar situation. They both work illegally in a hotel. They get £1.50 an hour, way below the rate paid to other staff. As a consequence, they work long hours to earn enough to live. Maria fled to Britain after her parents and siblings disappeared. She believes them to have been executed as political prisoners. Her family had been politically active at a time when war in her country was at its peak. Maria herself was raped twice by Serbian soldiers.

Maria is extremely unhappy with her current situation. She wants to apply for refugee status, but does not know who to turn to, and she is fearful that she will be returned home if she is found out. Maria has nothing to return to and fears for her life if she goes back.

SPECIFIC ACTIVITIES

1 What are Maria's rights?
2 What organisations exist to help people in Maria's situation? How do they operate, who funds them, and what are their aims and objectives?
3 What would Maria have to do to gain refugee status?

Scenario 7: David

David is 4 years old and was born with Down's syndrome. David, his parents June and Peter, and his older sister Kate, live in a semi-detached house in a small village.

Peter works offshore and is often away for long periods of time. June does not drive. David attends playgroup three times a week. The playgroup has been allocated an additional worker paid for by Social Services in order to ensure that both David and the other children get the care and education they need. David has difficulty communicating his needs, which can result in temper tantrums. He frequently wets himself and finds it very hard to wait his turn. He is quite demanding of adult attention.

David will shortly be starting school. His parents want him to go to the school in the next village so that he can get on the school bus with Kate. Kate is not so happy about this as she feels it will interrupt her play with her friends. Some parents at the school have made it known they are unhappy for David to attend the school. They feel he will take up too much of the teachers' time. The Education Department is suggesting that David go to a special school in the town some 39 miles distant. It argues that the village school, with only two classrooms and a teaching head, is unable to give David the educational experience he needs.

SPECIFIC ACTIVITIES

1 Find out about the Code of Practice for Children with Special Needs. What is the Education Department's responsibility under the statementing procedures?
2 What are the benefits and disadvantages of David attending the local school?
3 What are the benefits and disadvantages of David attending a special school?
4 Wherever possible, children with special needs should be integrated into mainstream schools. What would need to be made available to the school for David to be able to attend there?
5 What welfare benefits are David and his family entitled to?
6 How could the school deal with the fears of local parents?

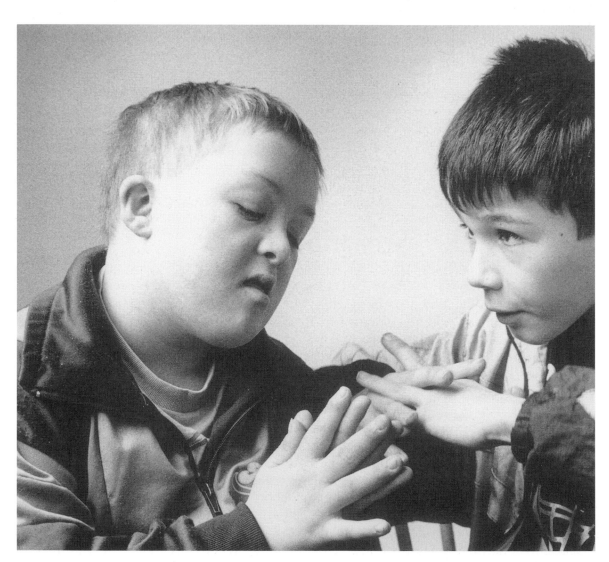

A young person with Down's syndrome

Scenario 8: Marcus

Marcus is 23 years old. He is currently living in a special unit for spine-injured people. Marcus was involved in a car accident that resulted in his becoming paralysed from the waist down. He also lost one of his legs below the knee. Marcus is still receiving medical care. He has physiotherapy every day. The staff are less concerned about Marcus's physical state than they are about his mental attitude. Marcus is extremely depressed. He is prone to violent mood swings and spends much of his time alone. The staff have had little success in engaging Marcus in occupational or rehabilitation therapy.

The unit is highly specialised and costly. Marcus has progressed as far as possible with his treatment, and his bed is needed. His doctors maintain that he can access the continued care he needs as an outpatient. His lack of co-operation in occupational and rehabilitation therapy add weight to the doctors' assessment that all has been done by the unit that can be done. Resources just don't allow Marcus to stay.

Marcus's only alternative is to be returned home. Both his parents work full time. His brother and sister have left home. Just prior to the accident, Marcus was about to start work. He had completed a degree in Information Technology and was top of the class in computer programming. He had found himself a flat that he planned to share with his girlfriend. She had been killed in the same accident. The accident happened on the way home from a varsity rugby match in which Marcus had scored the winning try.

Since the accident, many of Marcus's friends have been put off visiting him because of his attitude: often he won't speak to them.

SPECIFIC ACTIVITIES

You are Marcus's best friend. You went to school and then university together. You have tried your best to stick with him through what you know must be a really bad time. You know you are going to have to deal with Marcus very sensitively.

1 You make a list of how you think Marcus is feeling, and why.

2 You feel that Marcus needs counselling, even though he refused this at the hospital. You approach the various organisations that support people through accidents and bereavement, making notes and collecting leaflets so that you can pass this information on to Marcus when he is ready.

3 You know Marcus loves sport, and so you find out about the sports opportunities for the disabled available in the area.

4 You also find out about local self-help and support groups that might be able to introduce Marcus to other people so that he may learn from their experiences.

5 You find out what benefits Marcus is entitled to.

6 You know that Marcus is a talented computer programmer who could easily work from home, and you yourself have some ideas about what kind of business you and Marcus could run from home. You need to find out what help is available to set up in business

for yourselves. You decide to investigate, and you contact:
- the Prince's Trust
- the local Training and Enterprise Council (TEC)
- the Enterprise Council
- the Department of Trade and Industry
- your bank/building society.

Assignment

Title: Bidding for Funding.

Aim: to enable participants to undertake research, using a variety of study and key skills, in order to produce a sound business plan.

Learning outcomes: at the end of this assignment, the participant will:

- understand the process involved in bidding for funding
- have designed a viable project against the criteria provided
- have produced a business plan.

ASSIGNMENT BRIEF

This assignment requires you to design a project and produce a business plan that supports your chosen project idea.

The criteria for funding

Your project idea must be able to demonstrate how it will achieve at least two of the following if it is to receive funding. The funding available will only meet 50 per cent of the project's cost.

- Create or maintain employment;
- enhance the employment opportunities of disadvantaged groups such as the homeless, the disabled, lone parents, women, those threatened with redundancy or people under 25 years of age;
- enhance the regeneration of a community in need;
- offer training/vocational guidance;
- enhance the lives of a specific target group, eg children, older people, disabled people, children with special needs, lone parents, teenage parents, the terminally ill.

TASK 1: DECIDING ON YOUR PROJECT IDEA

Sketch out some ideas, and map them against the project criteria. This is best done in a group. You will need to think carefully about the ideas and how realistic they would be in the real, not a fictitious, world.

You will need to decide what kind of organisation is best placed to lead the proposed project, eg a statutory, private or voluntary organisation or a partnership arrangement.

As only 50 per cent funding is available, you will have to decide if the organisation will meet the other 50 per cent or if you are going to have *match funders*. These are organisations that fund the project either in cash or in kind alongside the lead organisation. For example: funding by bid: 50 per cent; Social Services: 25 per cent; District Council: 15 per cent; and Age Concern: 10 per cent.

Once you have done this, you will need to construct a *business plan*.

TASK 2: CONSTRUCTING YOUR BUSINESS PLAN

You will need to complete a business plan that includes the following. You will need to make up the detail, but the important thing is that you go through the process.

Part 1: the organisational background

Please give details of the organisation leading the bid for funding:

- name, address and telephone, fax and e-mail numbers
- the contact person and job title
- a brief account of the main activities of the lead organisation
- the number of employees in the lead organisation
- details of any partner organisations involved in the project.

Part 2: the proposed project

Please cover these points in full:

- the project name
- the geographical area covered by the project
- the aims and objectives of the project
- how the aims and objectives meet the funding criteria
- what the target group(s) is (are)
- evidence to support your proposal – how do you know this project is needed?

Part 3: an overview of the project

Please describe your project. Include a statement concerning equality of opportunity and managing diversity.

Part 4: project organisation

- How will the project be managed?
- How will the project be staffed?
- How will you ensure quality?
- How will you monitor and evaluate the project?
- How will you market the project?
- How will you ensure that you work in partnership with other appropriate organisations/persons?
- How will you establish links/networks in the local community?
- How will you identify and contact the target group?
- What is your exit strategy (ie what will happen at the end of the project)?

Part 5: project outcomes

Make a general statement about the benefits of the project. Identify specific outcomes, eg 6 × people employed in a community art gallery, 700 hours of training undertaken, 1 × community network meeting a month, or 1 × newsletter published every three months.

Part 6: financial information

Give a detailed breakdown of costs under the following headings:

- capital costs;
- revenue costs:
  - staff
  - travel
  - project materials (eg stationery, paper, pens)

- project equipment (eg computer, fax, photocopier)
- running costs (eg heat, light, telephone bills, postage)
- publicity (eg leaflets, photocopying)
- other (this will be dependent on the nature of your particular project).

Part 7: conclusion, acknowledgements and bibliography

A conclusion is a brief summary at the end of your report that draws together the main points that you make. It should not contain new material or argue your case.

Acknowledgements should be made when you use primary sources. You may wish to thank individuals or organisations for their help with your work. They are particularly relevant when their input cannot be recorded in the bibliography.

You need to decide which style of bibliography you are going to use: Harvard or numeric. Your bibliography and referencing should be true to one or the other and not a mixture of both.

activity

Find out how to use both of the above ways of styling a bibliography and references. You can consult a Study Skills booklet to obtain this information.

AND FINALLY . . .

All this was no easy task . . . so well done!

BIBLIOGRAPHY

Abel Smith, M. and Titmuss, K. (eds) (1974) *Richard M. Titmuss: Social Policy: An Introduction*, London: Allen and Unwin.

Abercrombie, N., Hill, S. and Turner, B. S. (1986) *Dictionary of Sociology*, Harmondsworth: Penguin Books.

Abercrombie, N., Warde, A. et al. (1988) *Contemporary British Society*, Cambridge: Polity Press.

Ackroyd, S. and Hughes, J. (1983) *Data Collection in Context*, Harlow: Longman.

Banting, K. C. (1979) *Poverty, Politics and Policy*, London: Macmillan.

Barnett, C. (1986) *The Audit of War*, London: Macmillan.

Bayley, R., Condy, A. and Ceridwen, R. (eds) (1994) *Policies for Families: Work Poverty and Resources*, London: Family Policy Studies Centre.

British Social Attitudes Survey (14th Report) (1997/8 edn), Ashgate Press.

Brown, M. (1985) *Introduction to Social Administration in Britain*, 6th edn, London: Hutchinson.

Brown, M. and Payne, S. (1994) *Introduction to Social Administration in Britain*, London: Routledge.

Bruyn, S. (1966) *The Human Perspective in Sociology: The Methodology of Participant Observation*, Englewood Cliffs, NJ: Prentice-Hall.

Bryson, L. (1992) *Welfare and the State: Who Benefits?*, London: Macmillan.

Bulmer, M. (ed) (1978) *Social Policy Research*, London: Macmillan.

Bulmer, M. (1982) *The Uses of Social Research: Social Investigation in Public Policy-making*, London: Allen and Unwin.

Christensen, D. (1998) 'Tamoxifen is not for every woman, government cautions', in *Medical News*, 4 June 1998.

Coates, D. (1984) *The Context of British Politics*, London: Hutchinson.

Crewe, I. (1987) 'A new class of politics', *The Guardian*, 15 June 1987.

Crystal, D. (1993) *Cambridge Paperback Encyclopedia*, Cambridge: Cambridge University Press.

DeBell, D. and Everett, J. (1997) *In a Class Apart: A Study of School Nursing*, Norwich: The Research Centre, Norwich City College.

Department for Education and Employment (1998) *New Ambitions for Our Country: a New Contract for Welfare*, London: DfEE.

Durkheim, E. (1970) *Suicide: A Study in Sociology*, London: Routledge & Kegan Paul.

European Commission (1997) *Demographic Report: Employment and Social Affairs Social Protection and Social Action*, Luxembourg: EUROP.

EUROPS (1997) *Demographic Trends in the EU*, Luxembourg: EUROPS.

Finch, J. (1993) 'It's great to have someone to talk to: ethics and politics of interviewing women', in Hammersley, M. (ed) *Social Research*, London: Sage.

Ford, R., Marsh, A. et al. (1998) *What Happens to Lone Parents: a Cohort Study 1991–1995*, Norwich: The Stationery Office.

Ford, R. and Millar, J. (1997) *Private Lives and Public Responses*, Grantham Books.

Frazer, D. (1985) *The Evolution of the Welfare State*, London: Macmillan.

George, V. and Wilding, P. (1985) *Ideology and Social Welfare*, London: Routledge & Kegan Paul.

Gladstone, D. (1996) *British Social Welfare: Past, Present and Future*, London: UCL Press.

Glaser, B. and Strauss, A. (1967) *The Discovery of Grounded Theory*, Chicago: Aldine Publishing.

Glennerster, H. (1995) *British Social Policy Since 1945*, Oxford: Blackwell.

Goffman, E. (1963) *Stigma*, Harmondsworth: Penguin Books.

Hammersley, M. (1995) *The Politics of Social Research*, London: Sage.

Hammersley, M. and Atkinson, P. (1993) *Ethnography: Principles in Practice*, London: Routledge.

Hantrais, L. (1997) *Social Policy in the European Union*, London: Macmillan.

Haralambos, M. and Holborn, J. (1991) *Sociology: Themes and Perspectives*, London: HarperCollins.

Hasler, F., Zarb, G. et al. (1998) *Key issues for Local Authority Implementation of Direct Payments*, London: PSI.

Help the Aged (1987) *An Ageing Population: Fact Sheet 2*, London: Family Policy Studies Centre.

Henwood, M. (1990) *Community Care and Elderly People*, London: Family Policy Studies Centre.

Hill, M. (1995) *Understanding Social Policy*, 4th edn, Oxford: Blackwell.

Hill, M. (1996) *Social Policy: A Comparative Analysis*, Englewood Cliffs, NJ: Prentice-Hall.

Hill, M. and Bramley, G. (1986) *Analysing Social Policy*, Oxford: Blackwell.

Holden, C., Meggitt, C., Collard, D. and Rycroft, C. (1996) *Further Studies for Social Care*, London: Hodder & Stoughton.

Home Office (1991) *Digest of Information on the Criminal Justice System*, London: Home Office.

Humphreys, L. (1970) *Tearoom Trade: Impersonal Sex in Public Places*, Chicago: Aldine Publishing.

Jowell, R., Park, A. et al. (1997) *British Social Attitudes – the 14th Report*, Aldershot: Ashgate Publishing.

Kavanagh, D. (1989) *British Politics: Continuities and Change*, Oxford: Oxford University Press.

Lovell, T. and Yeo, A. (1998) *Sociology for Childhood Studies*, London: Hodder & Stoughton.

Lynch, M. (1992) *Scotland: A New History*, London: Pimlico.

May, T. (1994) *Social Research Issues, Methods, Process*, Buckingham: Open University Press.

Mazey, S. (1992) *European Community Social Policy: Developments and Issues*, PNL Press.

McCarthy, M. (1989) *The New Politics of Welfare: An Agenda for the 1990s?*, London: Macmillan.

Mercer, D. (1988) *Chronicle of the 20th Century*, Harlow: Longman.

Newby, H. (1977) 'In the field: reflections on the study of Suffolk farm workers', in Bell, C. and Newby, H. (eds) *Doing Sociological Research*, London: Allen & Unwin.

Oliver, M. (1996) *Understanding Disability: From Theory to Practice*, London: Macmillan.

Open University, Block 8, *Evaluation of Research, DE304*, Buckingham: Open University Press.

Pharmaceutical Information Associates, 'Breast Cancer and the Tamoxifen Trials', *Medical Sciences Bulletin*, August 1994.

Robertson, D. (1985) *Dictionary of Politics*, Harmondsworth: Penguin Books.

Roll, J. (1990) *Young People: Growing Up in the Welfare State*, London: Family Policy Studies Centre.

Roney, A. (1998) *EC/EU Fact Book: A Complete Question and Answer Guide*, London: Kogan Page.

Spiker, P. (1995) *Social Policy: Themes and Approaches*, Englewood Cliffs, NJ: Prentice-Hall.

Thomas, P. (1985) *The Aims and Outcomes of Social Policy Research*, Croom Helm.

Williams, F. (1994) *Social Policy: A Critical Introduction*, Cambridge: Polity Press.

Williams, R. and Lamb, M. (1997) *European Social Policy Fact Sheet*, Norwich: The Stationery Office.

GLOSSARY

Action research An investigation which is used to inform practice in an ongoing manner.

Administrators These exist at all levels of an organisation, from directors to managers. They are concerned with the development and implementation of policy and service provision.

Advocacy Acting or speaking on behalf of another, or supporting someone to speak for themselves.

Altruism The principle of unselfish regard for the needs and interests of others.

Anthropologist Someone who studies humans, their origins, institutions, beliefs and behaviour.

Attitudinal survey A survey which discovers what people think about an issue.

Bevan, Aneurin A Labour MP in the 1940s, who worked with the British Medical Association in order to secure the necessary agreements from doctors that paved the way for the 1946 National Health Service Act.

Beveridge, Sir William (1879–1963) A Liberal and often called the founding father of the welfare state. In the 1940s, he was responsible for introducing the system of social security that still informs the way we organise both the benefit system and job centres today.

Butler, R. A. A Conservative MP in the 1940s who managed to persuade the Church to agree to changes in the school curriculum which led to the 1944 Education Act.

Census An official periodic count of a population.

Charter A written document that grants certain rights and privileges.

Code of conduct An agreed set of rules of behaviour.

Collectivism Working for the good of society/community not the individual.

Community care A policy, underpinned by legislation, that attempts to provide various kinds of services that support the care of people in the community.

Control group A group with the same characteristics as the experimental group, but where there is no intervention, enabling the researcher to compare the two groups.

Decentralisation Removing control of service responsibility from government and its departments to smaller geographical areas (divisions) or organisations (schools).

Devolution Transfer of authority from central to regional government.

Egalitarianism This holds that all citizens of a state should be afforded exactly the same rights and privileges (equal opportunities).

Empiricism A philosophy which holds that knowledge derives from experience, and is measured through the collection of social facts in the same way as sound or distance are measured.

Empowerment Taking or being given power, the act of being given or taking control of our own life or of issues that directly affect it.

Equality of opportunity The belief that all citizens should be treated with equal respect. Equality is not about everyone having to be the same, or treated the same. Equal opportunity acknowledges cultural differences and lifestyle choices.

Equal opportunities policy This describes a specific set of measures adopted by an organisation that demonstrate how it will ensure equality and deal with discrimination.

Ethnography This holds that people interpret the world and act according to their own socially constructed meanings.

European Parliament Elected from Member States, this can call on the European

Commission to prepare legislation, and it is consulted on proposals.

European Social Fund The European Union's financial instrument to improve employment through vocational training and job creation.

European Union The name given to the European Economic Community in the Treaty of the European Union 1992.

Evaluation An exercise which measures whether or not the subject evaluated has met its objective.

Explanatory survey A survey which is designed to test theories.

Factual survey This describes the characteristics of a population.

Field research Research which takes place in the heart of the environment of a group of people being studied.

Formative evaluation An evaluation method which measures the ongoing processes of the subject evaluated.

Guidance Regulations that should take into account certain requirements or ways of doing things.

Ideology A set of ideas and opinions.

Ideology of welfare A set of ideas and opinions that describe a society's beliefs and opinions about, and attitudes towards, its welfare services.

Informal sector Care given by family, relatives or friends with no professional interest.

Institutional welfare This advocates a central role for the state in providing welfare services.

Keynesianism This describes an economic theory which held that governments could control the economy by controlling public spending.

Labour exchanges Now called Job Centres, these are places people go to find out about the jobs available in their area and/or schemes to help them find work.

Labour Party A British political organisation, traditionally adhering to socialist ideologies, and more recently adhering to principles that underpin a mixed economy of welfare.

Laissez-faire This maintains that industries and businesses should be allowed to trade freely without restrictions or quotas.

Lobbyist Someone who tries to influence legislation on behalf of a particular interest.

Mandate Official.

Mandatory regulation A requirement that must be carried out (ie no choice).

Market research The study of the influences on customer behaviour, and the analysis of market characteristics and trends.

Mission statement A written statement that outlines an organisation's goal or aims and objectives.

Mixed economy of welfare This describes the provision of services where the government takes responsibility for some things but also encourages private- and voluntary-sector intervention.

Model This means something worthy of imitation. A model represents a framework upon which to build ideas.

Monetarism This is an economic theory that holds that governments should not interfere with market forces but should instead allow the business economy to find its own balance. The government's role should be to keep down inflation.

National Curriculum Legislation and guidelines that dictate what is taught in schools to children age 5 and upwards.

Nationalisation This is the policy of taking firms, enterprises or whole industries into public ownership. Utilities such as gas, electricity, coal and the railways were nationalised in the 1940s and 1950s. They were then denationalised in the 1980s and 1990s. It is a policy that is no longer popular.

New social movement The organised action of a group to promote social interests often of disadvantaged groups.

Non-probability Sampling methods where there is an unknown probability of selection.

Official statistics Statistics collected by or on behalf of government agencies.

Opinion poll The canvassing of a representative sample of people on a question to find out the general opinion.

People's Budget The budget of 1909

introduced in the British Parliament by the then British Prime Minister Lloyd George. The budget raised the taxes of those on higher incomes, and was seen to favour the working class.

Permissive regulation A requirement that may be carried out (ie some choice).

Phenomenologist Someone who believes that the social world is constructed through the meanings given to it by individuals.

Political ideology A set of ideas and opinions that describe how a society should organise itself and allocate its resources.

Positivism The objective collection of social facts through experiments and observations to test a theory of knowledge.

Pressure group A group which campaigns and lobbies on a specific issue.

Primary legislation European law based on international acts and treaties.

Private sector Organisations funded by private means: businesses, companies etc.

Probability sampling methods Sampling methods where there is a known probability of selection which can be statistically tested.

Public sector State-funded provision.

Purposive sampling methods Sampling methods where there is an unknown probability of selection.

Qualitative research An investigation which aims to understand the kind of subject being studied.

Quantitative research An investigation which measures the subject by amount.

Questionnaire A set of questions on a form, submitted to a number of people to collect statistical information.

Referendum A vote of the electorate on an issue of importance.

Regulation Directly enforceable European law, binding on Member States.

Sample A group of individuals selected from a population to represent the views and behaviour of the whole population.

Sampling frame A group which is representative of the population being studied.

Secondary legislation European law based on acts passed to ensure that the treaties are applied.

Secondary sources Data which has already been collected by other research projects, administrative sources or other means.

Self-help A doctrine first introduced by Samuel Smiles in 1859. It is the belief that people benefit more from doing things for themselves, rather than having things done for them by others, eg by the government via welfare services.

Social administrator A professional who has a role in the organisation, monitoring and delivery of services in the public sector.

Social Chapter An annex to the Maastricht Treaty on the European Union Agreement on Social Policy.

Social Charter An agreement by 11 Member States of the European Union in 1989 on a range of social issues.

Social coherence The term initiated by Jacques Delor to describe how European Union countries should develop consistency in social systems.

Social engineering This describes law, policy, attitudes, opinions and cultural norms that dictate what is considered acceptable and unacceptable in society.

Social insurance Insurance schemes which can provide members with a range of social welfare provision including health care and care for the elderly.

Socialist A person who believes in socialism. The ideology of socialism holds that the state should regulate key businesses, industries (the province of capitalists) and services, thus ensuring access to wealth and the redistribution of wealth to the less well off (ie the working class) in society.

Social policy The term used to describe any government-led policy that regulates the organisation and delivery of services or resource allocation in the society in which it has been developed.

Social problem A situation that is difficult to deal with or understand.

Social research An investigation to collect information about the social world.

Social Security Now called Income Support, this is the payment of benefits to those in need.

Social worker A trained employee of

organisations providing personal social services.

Sociology The study of social relationships, social interaction, how society functions and how a society organises itself. A sociologist is a person who undertakes sociological research.

Statement of intent This clearly describes what an institution, organisation or agency has decided it is going to do about a given aspect of its operation.

Statism This holds that the state has an obligation to intervene in any matter that may undermine the welfare of its citizens.

Statutory agencies Agencies run by the state, ie local government, health authorities, the police etc.

Statutory service One that must be provided under the law.

Summative evaluation An evaluation method which measures the final outcomes and achievements of the subject evaluated.

Sustainability The capacity of something to be maintained on a continuous basis without depleting natural resources.

Thatcherism An ideology based on the policies introduced by Margaret Thatcher during her term as British Prime Minister between 1979 and 1990.

Titmuss, Richard An eminent writer in the field of social policy and social administration. His essays on war, the theory of reciprocity and the gift relationship are often used to explain the evolution of the welfare state.

Trade union An organised collective of working people, usually united by occupational or service interests.

Unionism The collective voice of the workforce through individual membership of a union.

Unit of analysis The single subject of the group being studied.

Universalism This maintains that all citizens have an equal right to free and accessible services provided by the state.

Utilitarianism A doctrine first introduced by Jeremy Bentham in the 1830s. It believed that law (and policy) should reflect the 'greatest good for the greatest number of people'.

Voluntary sector A collection of non-profit organisations, some of which have charity status.

Welfare This is generally taken to mean well-being. Social policy is concerned with the well-being of society. Welfare services provide for the well-being of those using them.

Welfare pluralism This is the provision of services from many different sources. See **mixed economy of welfare**.

Welfare state This refers to areas of service provision that the government has a role in funding, planning and regulating. Traditionally, these have been health, education, income maintenance, housing and personal social services.

INDEX